Fluberbia

No Prep: Novel Unit

by Elizabeth Chapin-Pinotti

© 2015 Elizabeth Chapin-Pinotti – Fluberbia: No Prep Novel Unit
ISBN-13: 978-0692457146

Lucky Jenny Publishing, Inc.
Lucky Willy Imprint
P.O. Box 331
Plymouth, CA 95669
www.luckyjenny.com

Table of Contents

Introduction

In order to prepare students for life and work in the 21st Century we must infuse them with curiosity about how and why things work, we must teach them to think both creatively and critically, to work together, to communicate their ideas and to embrace the fact that math, science, technology and engineering are infused in every part of our lives. To do this successfully, students must be provided with project-based learning opportunities that incorporate academic and technological skills that necessitate students with different aptitudes, backgrounds and ideas to work together.

This book is a companion to <u>Fluberbia</u>. It can be taught as a read aloud infused with lessons. Or teachers may wish to purchase one workbook per student – that is inclusive of the novel or one novel per student so they may read on their own or in groups and then work together on assignments. There is no wrong way to teach this book.

This book provides learn-by-doing work that encourages student cognitive development and meets imperative 21st Century learning and Common Core State Standards benchmarks. Learning-by-doing in a project-based environment provides the perfect setting for students to gain a deeper understanding of content as they incorporate collaboration, communication, critical thinking, creativity and digital learning. Project-based learning also allows for immediate and authentic assessment of what students are learning and what needs to be reinforced. Monitor and adjusting lessons and instruction is built in.

This novel unit also contains three Performance Tasks similar to those found in the new computer adaptive testing. Some of the Performance Tasks will be aligned to English Language Arts Standards (ELA). The ELA Performance Tasks focus on reading, writing, speaking and listening and research claims. They measure capacities such as depth of understanding, interpretive and analytical ability, basic recall, synthesis and research. They make take place over time.

Some Performance Tasks will be aligned to the math CCSS. Math Performance Tasks will:
- Integrate knowledge and skills across multiple claims.
- Measure capacities such as depth of understanding, research skills, and/or complex analysis with relevant evidence.
- Require student-initiated planning, management of information/data and ideas, and/or interaction with other materials.
- Reflect a real-world task and/or scenario-based problem.

Item Types
- Represent content that is relevant and meaningful to students.
- Allow for demonstration of important knowledge and skills.
- Require scoring that focuses on the essence of the claim(s) for which the task was written.
- Allow for multiple approaches.
- Seem feasible for the school/classroom environment.

The project-based STEM activities cover both physical and biological sciences. Each activity contains instructions, background information tied to the story, a list of necessary materials and a vocabulary list. It is important to remember to use these STEM activities as learning opportunities by allowing group work and asking questions that foster both creative and critical thinking, such as: "what if we tired...", "how might we do it differently..." and "what could be done differently to...". Students must be encouraged to turn their ideas into reality. Teachers must remember that it is not always about the right answer, but about the problem exploration.

Vocabulary for 21st Century Teachers

21st Century Vocabulary			
analyze	apply	arrange	assess
believe	share	preserve	engage
brainstorm	build	challenge	chart
collaborate	communicate	complete	consider
create	critique	design	develop
discover	discuss	dramatize	evaluate
graph	gather	imagine	implement
improve	incorporate	improvise	initiate
innovate	inquire	invent	investigate
listen	model	organize	plan
practice	relate	research	review
support	synthesize	seek	wonder
demonstrate	self-assess	peer	respect

Before You Begin:

Plot Overview: Twelve-year-old Janie and her younger brother Jake are visiting their Zia and Zio in the Sierra Nevada Foothills of California. It is between Christmas and New Year and Janie, Jake and Zia spend the day exploring the small gold country town, playing games and wandering the grounds of the old lodge building that sits across the street from Zia's house. Zia is Italian for aunt.

The day is crystal clear, but billowy clouds are backing up in the sky and it looks like a storm is brewing. From the brown winter ground-cover, Jake notices something green growing. He wants to pick it, but Zia stops him and wonders aloud if it may snow – foreshadowing the events about to unfold.

Janie has trouble sleeping that night. A light from across the street catches her eye. It is coming from the flower. She goes outside to get a better look and sees that a violet is growing. She bends down to get a good whiff, but something is not right. She feels like she is falling – and she is – through the flower. She whirls and twirls and lands in the enchanted Kingdom of Fluberbia.

In Fluberbia, Jane meets the twin princesses, Julia and Claire and discovers that they were waiting for her to help them rescue their parents from the tower they were put in by the evil Empress Ephora—who is also their aunt. Julia is a fairy princess – due to a curse. The girls are charming, delightful, brave and strong.

After a breakfast, that that literally slithers, Janie and Claire approach Miloph, their friendly bird friend, for he has the parchment that will map out their journey to save the King and Queen of Fluberbia. The parchment turns out to be one in a series of riddles the girls must solve in order to fill Ephora's Crown of Goodness and save the King and Queen.

Theme: It is imperative for students to understand that a theme is the lesson or moral underlying the plot. The plot is what happens, the theme is a book's opinion about life, human nature or elements of society.

Themes of Fluberbia:

1. **Overcoming Adversity:** Overcoming adversity is the main theme in Fluberbia. Overcoming adversity means that characters are put in difficult situations and find a way to come out on time. They defy odds. In Fluberbia, twelve-year-old Janie is spending the night at her aunt's house in December. This night turns out to be a very special night – which Janie discovers when she falls through a violet and lands in the Kingdom of Fluberbia – where she helps two young, smart, strong princesses overcome many obstacles to save their parents and get Janie back home again.
2. **Hero Within:** Janie and the two princesses, Claire and Julia, are young and small, but they are forced into a situation that draws on their inner strengths to succeed.
3. **Good vs. Evil:** Good vs. evil is present both externally and internally as the girls must stand against the princesses' evil aunt to save their parents and return Janie home.

Main Characters:

Janie: Janie is a twelve-year-old from California. She is bright, funny and a bit sarcastic. She is the girl next door in the making. She is braver than she knows and finds out that her family has a special connection to a faraway land of another earth.

Claire: The Princess Claire is three years younger than Janie. She is the daughter of the true and rightful ruler of the Kingdom of Fluberbia. She accompanies Janie on her quest.

Julia: The Princess Julia is Claire's twin, only she is blessed/cursed with the magic of the kingdom, something her parents tried to spread between the girls and helped to cause the whole parents in the tower thing. Julia can transform into a fairy princess – only she doesn't quite have a handle on her magic yet.

Teaching Fluberbia

Fluberbia can be read aloud with students following along, read aloud to students, read in groups or pairs or just about any way you desire. The chapters are divided with lessons and assignments following each, so they can be printed in packets and assigned to students. Printing chapter by chapter packets are 8.5 x 11; however, included in Appendix B is the novel divided by section and may be printed in booklets.

The center activities that following in the Appendix are intended to engage students and supplement the chapter activities – which include Common Core State Standards for the 3, 4 and 5th grade span. Any of the end-of-chapter activities may also be used as center activities. This unit is designed to be cross-curricular and incorporates STEM, social studies, math and, of course, centers around English Language Arts.

The activities lend themselves to differentiation. Comprehension checks accompany the chapters and the final assessment is by way of an interactive assignment. I use the Interactive Notebook as a final assessment for students. Any of the end-of-chapter work may also be added to student Interactive Notebooks.

The novel **FLUberBiᗡ** is available through Lucky Jenny Publishing, at books stores and at amazon.com, but the novel is included herein and does not need to be purchased. Some find it more cost effective to purchase a classroom set of novels. Also, available is the **FLUberBiᗡ** Interactive Reader – a workbook the requires no copying. This can be purchased directly by contacting publisher@luckyjenny.com. The cost, inclusive of shipping, is $150 for a class set of 30. This workbooks requires no copying and may be more cost effective.

Happy Reading!!

Chapter 1: The Magic Flower

The day before it happened was one of those crystal clear days, when the sky is as blue as the Hawaiian ocean, and the puffs of clouds are sparse, but giant and fluffy, perfect cotton ball visions floating overhead – soft, slow and bouncy.

Janie and Jake were visiting Zia. They ran all over town – from park to park – playing pirates and sea captain and house and hide and seek and warrior and adventurer and army and tag and doctor and scientist.

They explored the alleys and the old town at the fairgrounds. They even went up to Lodge Hill, though they'd always heard it was haunted. The ground around the decaying, dilapidated building was barren – except for three bright green plants peeking through the golden dry grass of the impending winter.

"Look Zia," Janie ran up to them. "Something's growing."

"Let's pick one and take it home," Jake said, bending to see a tiny purple bloom starting to bud.

"No, no," Zia said, leaning over the plant to examine it closely. "That's a special plant. It has to stay here."

Zia took a deep breath. It was December 28 and these were the plants. She knew what that meant. She looked up to the sky. "I wonder if it will snow?" she asked aloud.

"Oh, I hope so," Janie said, not knowing why Zia wanted it to snow but thinking it would be awesome if it did.

"It would be magical," Zia said, almost to herself. She smiled at her niece and nephew. "And then you would know."

"Know what?" they asked together.

"Never believe it. Not in a million years. We'll just have to wait and see," Zia said, walking back towards the house.

Janie had a hard time sleeping that night. The moon was gone and a deafening silence overtook the darkness. There were no nighttime sounds, no leaves rustling in the soft wintery wind. Just silence.

Jake was sleeping soundly next to her...as he always did when he was at Zia's, all stretched out, covers wrapped around him mummy-like and, of course, hogging the bed.

"Oh well," Janie sighed to herself. "I can't sleep anyway."

She climbed out of bed and lovingly flicked her little brother's ear. He breathed a huffy puff and rolled over.

She pattered into Zio and Zia's room. Both sleeping, she thought.

And then she noticed it, out of the corner of her eye, by chance because it wasn't really that easy to see.

She walked to the big dormer window and tried to see over the fence to the tiny light glowing on Lodge Hill. She stood on her tippy toes and squinted, but she still couldn't see it.

She walked to the French doors that led to the pool and opened them. She pulled on the pink Uggs, cast aside on the screen porch after a day's play. They were cold. She shivered and grabbed one of the afghans thrown over the quilt rack.

She didn't see it until she got to the gate by Zio's truck.

Growing from one of the bright green plants, up by the lodge, was a beautiful, tiny purple flower that seemed to be emanating its own light.

She opened the gate slowly. It creaked and she jumped.

"Easy Janie," she said to herself as she closed it behind her to brave the dark of the street alone.

She looked both ways, even thought it was one o'clock in the morning and most normal people were asleep.

She felt something cold fall on her nose, then on her head, and again. She looked up and let out an excited scream as thousands of fluffy white snowflakes drifted through the air.

It was snowing. Through the white curtain, the light seemed to get brighter. It seemed to be calling her to its glow.

She ran across the street and up the hill. The flower was beautiful, perfectly purple and fragrant. She bent down to get a better whiff and her tummy started turning. She felt like she was slipping. She looked down and her hands were shrinking, her legs where shrinking, her whole body was shrinking. Then she felt the sensation of falling, like off of the waterfall on Splash Mountain at Disneyland.

She landed hard on her bottom, but on soft mossy ground. Only she wasn't in Plymouth anymore.

She was in a forest of sorts and standing above her were two very large men with eyes in both the front and back of their heads. And they had extra lips on the tops of their noggins. She'd never seen anything like it before in her life.

She was definitely not at Zia's anymore.

Performance Task 1
"Fluberbia Chapter 1: The Magic Flower"

Grade:	3
Claim:	1. Students can read closely and analytically to comprehend a range of increasingly complex literary and informational texts.
Assessment Target(s):	**Reasoning and Evidence:** Use supporting evidence to interpret and explain inferences about character traits, motivations, feelings, point of view, or author's lesson or message.
Secondary Target(s):	**Key Details:** Use explicit details and information from the text to support answers or basic inferences.
Standard(s):	RL-2, RL-3, RL -6 Secondary Standard(s): RL-1, RL-3
Difficulty	Medium
Item Type:	Constructed Response
Score Points:	3
Correct Response:	See rubric
Stimulus/Passage	Excerpt from "Chapter One: The Magic Flower"
Stimuli/Text Complexity	The quantitative measures are probably reflecting the complexity of the sentence structure. Every other element is simpler. Based on these sets of measures, this passage is recommended for assessment at grades 2 and 4.
Acknowledgement(s):	Source Title: Fluberbia Grade Band: 2-5 Author: Elizabeth Chapin-Pinotti
Item / Task Notes:	
How this item / task contributes to the sufficient evidence for this claim:	To complete this task, students must write an appropriate response and cite evidence to support an inference about a character in a literary text.
Target –Specific Attributes (e.g., accessibility issues):	Stimulus texts should be on grade levels. For CRs (Constructed Responses) on state tests, students will be required to enter text using a keyboard; hearing – or vision- impaired students may need alternate formats or support.

Stimulus Text:

Read this text and then answer the prompt that follows it.

Chapter One: The Magic Flower
From <u>Fluberbia</u>

Janie had a hard time sleeping that night. The moon was gone and a deafening silence overtook the darkness. There were no nighttime sounds, no leaves rustling in the soft wintery wind. Just silence.

Jake was sleeping soundly next to her...as he always did when he was at Zia's, all stretched out, covers wrapped around him mummy-like and, of course, hogging the bed.

"Oh well," Janie sighed to herself. "I can't sleep anyway."

She climbed out of bed and lovingly flicked her little brother's ear. He breathed a huffy puff and rolled over.

She pattered into Zio and Zia's room. Both sleeping, she thought.

And then she noticed it, out of the corner of her eye, by chance because it wasn't really that easy to see.

She walked to the big dormer window and tried to see over the fence to the tiny light glowing on Lodge Hill. She stood on her tippy toes and squinted, but she still couldn't see it.

She walked to the French doors that led to the pool and opened them. She pulled on the pink Uggs, cast aside on the screen porch after a day's play. They were cold. She shivered and grabbed one of the afghans thrown over the quilt rack.

She didn't see it until she got to the gate by Zio's truck.

Growing from one of the bright green plants, up by the lodge, was a beautiful, tiny purple flower that seemed to be emanating its own light.

She opened the gate slowly. It creaked and she jumped.

"Easy Janie," she said to herself as she closed it behind her to brave the dark of the street alone.

She looked both ways, even thought it was one o'clock in the morning and most normal people were asleep.

She felt something cold fall on her nose, then on her head, and again. She looked up and let out an excited scream as thousands of fluffy white snowflakes drifted through the air.

It was snowing. Through the white curtain, the light seemed to get brighter. It seemed to be calling her to its glow.

She ran across the street and up the hill. The flower was beautiful, perfectly purple and fragrant. She bent down to get a better whiff and her tummy started turning. She felt like she was slipping. She looked down and her hands were shrinking, her legs where shrinking, her whole body was shrinking. Then she felt the sensation of falling, like off of the waterfall on Splash Mountain at Disneyland.

She landed hard on her bottom, but on soft mossy ground. Only she wasn't in Plymouth anymore.

She was in a forest of sorts and standing above her were two very large men with eyes in both the front and back of their heads. And they had extra lips on the tops of their noggins. She'd never seen anything like it before in her life.

She was definitely not at Zia's anymore.

Item Prompt:

The author shows that Janie is a curious person. Write a paragraph telling how Janie is curious. Use specific details from the story to support your answer.

Name: _____ **Date:** _____

Use this template to organize your thoughts before you write your paragraph.

Performance Task Graphic Organizer	
Fluberbia: Chapter 1: The Magic Flower	
Main idea of your paragraph	
Evidence 1 showing Janie is curious	
Support for Evidence 1	
Evidence 2 showing Janie is curious	
Support for Evidence 2	
Evidence 3 showing Janie is curious	
Support for Evidence 3	
Conclusion	

Performance Task 1 Rubric

	Scoring Rubric
3	The response: • Gives sufficient evidence of student's ability to use supporting evidence to interpret and explain inferences about a character • Includes specific explanations that make reference to the text • Fully supports the interfaces with clearly relevant details from the text
2	The response: • Gives some evidence of the ability to use supporting evidence to interpret and explain inferences about a character. • Includes some specific explanations that make reference to the text. • Adequately supports the inferences with clearly relevant details from the text.
1	The response: • Gives limited evidence of the ability to use supporting evidence to interpret and explain inferences about a character • Includes specific explanations but they are not explicit or make only vague references to the text. • Supports the inferences with at least one detail but the relevance of that detail to the text must be inferred
0	The response: A response gets no credit if it provides no evidence of the ability to use supporting evidence to interpret and explain inferences about a character and includes no relevant information from the text.

STEM Tie-In Plant Growth Rate

In the afternoon, when Janie is walking with her Zia, aunt, and brother, they notice a tiny flower beginning to bloom. By the time night comes, the flower is fully grown and large enough for Janie to fall through – only the plant grew without light or heat.

In this experiment you will:
- Observe how the growth rate of a plant is affected by light
- Use a spreadsheet to enter plant growth data
- Display your data using a graph
- Brainstorm your way through the experimentation process
- Evaluate to check your finding.

Science: Students will understand the relationships between an organism and their physical environment. They will also learn that careful observation; peer brainstorming and simple experiments can lead to quantitative results.

Math: Students will use math as an analytical tool to pose questions, derive at answers and find solutions. Students will test and check to find the most appropriate operations to solve math problems and apply math skills to the real world.

Engineering: Students will work collaboratively to propose alternative procedures and solutions, use verbal and graphic techniques to present conclusions and to troubleshoot procedures and solutions.

Technology: Students will use simple spreadsheets to manipulation data and produce graphs and charts.

Materials:
- 2 containers per group
- 2 bean seeds per group
- Potting soil
- Markers
- Rulers in cms
- Masking tape

Vocabulary
> **Stem:** The part of the plant that carries food and water and holds the plan upright.
> **Leaf:** The part of the plant that collects light from the sun and produces food.
> **Roots:** The part of the plant that gets water and food from the soil.
> **Seed:** Seeds are made by flowers and can grow into new plants.
> **Germinate:** When a seed begins to grow and sprout.

Plant Growth Rate Experiment – Standards – NGSS 3 LS.1

Materials:
- 2 containers per group
- 2 bean seeds per group
- Potting soil
- Markers
- Rulers in cms
- Masking tape

Vocabulary	
stem	The part of the plant that carries food and water and holds the plan upright.
leaf	The part of the plant that collects light from the sun and produces food.
roots	The part of the plant that gets water and food from soil.
seeds	Seeds are made from by flowers and can grow into new plants.
germinate	When a seed begins to grow and sprout.

Procedure:
1. Read over this entire experiment packet.
2. Gather your materials.
3. Print your name or your group name on each cup.
4. Fill 2 cups or pots with potting soil.
5. Label cup 1: "Full Sunlight".
6. Label cup 2: "Dim Light".
7. Poke a hole in the potting soil in each cup, plant one seed in each cup.
8. Put one cup in full light and the other in a low light area.
9. Observe the pots each day. When the seeds begin to germinate, use your ruler to measure the height of each plant and record your data.
10. Make sure you measure your plants the same way each day.
11. Measure your plants and record your data for one week.

Questions While You Wait for Your Plant to Grow

Discuss the following questions in your group and summarize your discussions in the space provided.

1. Predict what will happen. Write your prediction. Return at the end of the experiment and check your prediction against what happened.

What I Predict	What Happened

2. On Day 3, Compare and Contrast "Full Sunlight" Plant and "Dim Light" Plant.

Full Sunlight Plant   Both   Dim Light Plant

3. Come up with an invention that will allow you to keep your plants side by side, but have one in full sunlight and one in dim or no light.

Name of Invention: _____

Invention Description: _____

_____

_____

_____

How Will Your Invention Work: _____

_____

_____

_____

Diagram of Your Invention:

Plant Growth Rate Data Table
Measurement in Centimeters

Plant Growth Rate		
Day	Height of Bean Plant in Full Light	Height of Bean Plant in Low Light
1		
2		
3		
4		
5		

Day 4 Drawing of Full Light Plant	Day 4 Drawing of Dim Light Plant

Lesson Learning Objectives
- Learn and use spreadsheet terms including columns, rows and cells
- Enter data into a spreadsheet
- Adjust column width
- Change style of data in cell
- Create and format a chart from data entered

The screenshots for this lesson are from MS Excel 10; however the lesson will work in most spreadsheet software including Google Docs, Open Office and iWorks.

Procedure

1. Open a new spreadsheet document.
   a. Notice that the columns are named using letters (A, B, C...)
   b. Notice that the rows are named using numbers (1,2,3...)
2. Put your mouse over the cell **A1** and type in the word "Days". This is your label.
3. Tap the **Tab** key (all the way left). The curser will move to **B1**.
4. In **B1** type in "Full Light Plant Height"
5. Widen column **B** so the label fits in to the cell. Use your mouse and put if over the line between letters B and **C**. When you are between click and drag the line until the words fit.

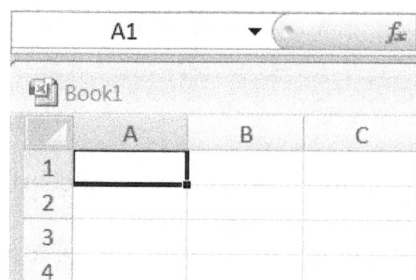

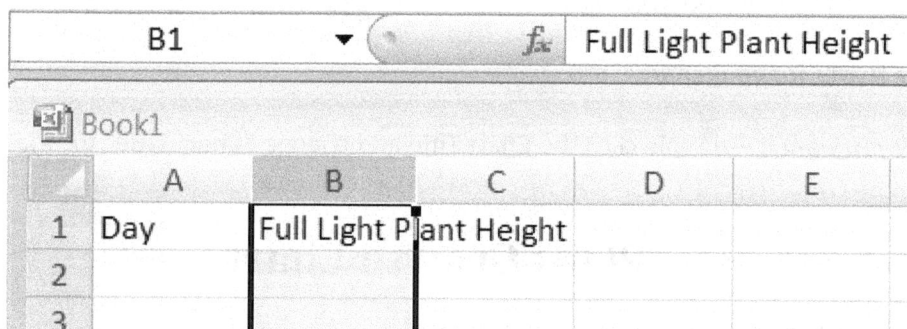

6. Hit the **Tab** key again and to go cell **C1** – what do you think you should type in...think about it..."Dim Light Plant Height"
7. Widen column **C** to fit your text.
8. Center your data: click on **A1** and drag your mouse over to **C1**. This will highlight all three boxes. Next hit the **Align Center** button to center your labels.

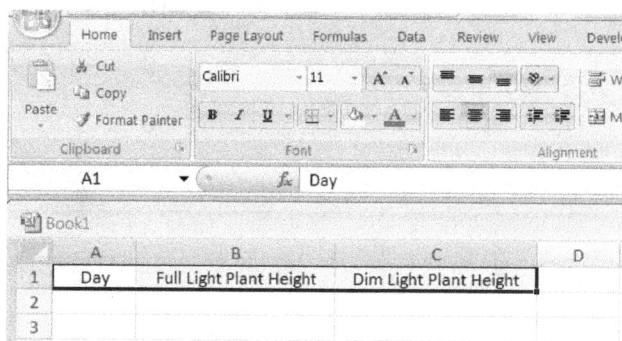

9. Enter the Day numbers in column **A**.

	A	B	C	D
1	Day	Full Light Plant Height	Dim Light Plant Height	
2	1			
3	2			
4	3			
5	4			
6	5			

10. Enter the data you gathered. Your spread sheet should match your hand written sheet.

	A	B	C	D
1	Day	Full Light Plant Height	Dim Light Plant Height	
2	1	3	2	
3	2	6	4	
4	3	8	5	
5	4	9	6	
6	5	12	8	

11. Now you will create your chart. Click on **A1**.

12. Find the **Insert** menu on the top of the screen.

13. Select a **Chart** – anyone you want. Play with them – selecting different ones. Be sure you choose one the makes your data sparkle! Click around to change the color and the settings of your chart. There is really nothing you can do to mess it up. Have fun playing with it.

14. If you do want to change something – just go it the little flippy arrow and you can undo anything. I call this key the "do over" key.

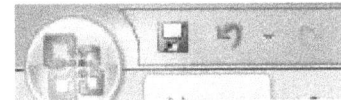

15. Find **Chart Layouts** and select a layout for your chart.

16. When the layout looks the way you want it – double click the Chart Title and change "**Chart Title**" to "**Plant Growth**"

17. Click **Save** and **Print**.

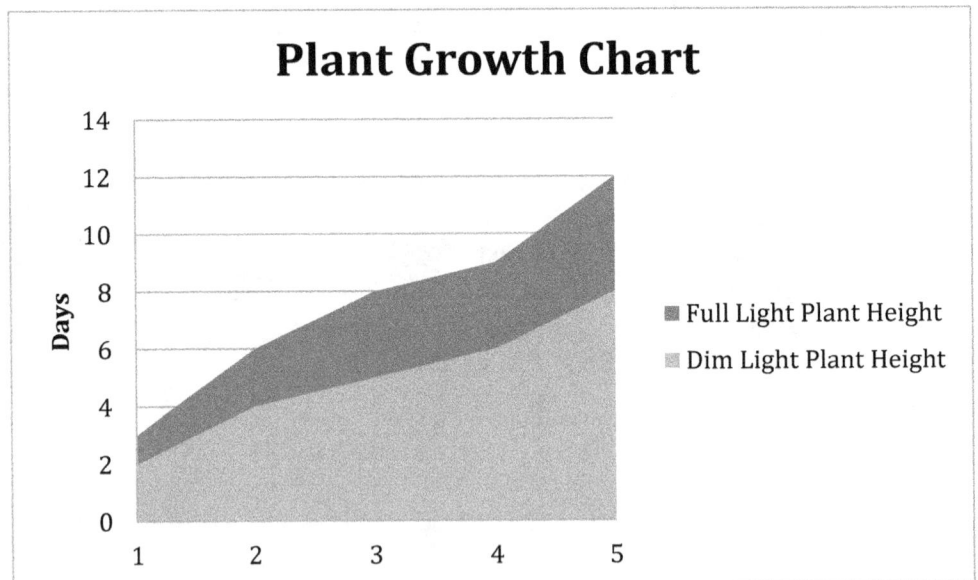

Plant Growth Chart

Name: _____ Date: _____ #: _____

Quick Write Comprehension – Constructed Response

1. What events lead up to Janie "not being at Zia's anymore"?

Event 1: _____
_____
_____
_____
_____

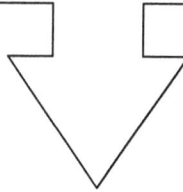

Event 2: _____
_____
_____
_____
_____

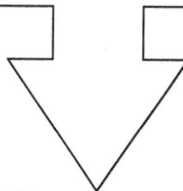

Event 3: _____
_____
_____
_____
_____

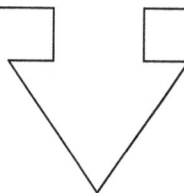

Name: _____ Date: _____ #: _____

Constructed Response Comprehension Questions

1. Describe the "day before it happened"? _____

_____

_____

2. What did Janie and Jake do with their Zia? _____

_____

_____

3. What was growing at the lodge: _____

_____

_____

_____

_____

4. Predict what you think will happen next: _____

_____

_____

_____

Chapter 2: Down to Fluberbia

She tried to stand, but the giants would not let her.

The tall men groaned at her and, without a word, plucked her from the ground and spun her around.

She noticed she was in a forest of sorts. Tall, towering trees cast shadows from the setting moon. And it was warm. The snow was gone and a summer breeze felt good on her shivering body.

"Put me down," she demanded, finding the courage to speak, "and please tell me where we are."

A light flashed before her and from out of the glowing moon-filled blackness leapt a small figure, with wings and a golden crown. Janie gasped.

"You are in Fluberbia," the beautiful creature spoke as she landed in front of the girl.

Janie could see she was a girl herself, a beautiful girl with brown hair and brown eyes and glowing wings and the best crown Janie had ever seen.

The creature walked all 360 degrees around Janie and back to the spot where she first floated. "You are not a Ephorian," she said finally.

"I most certainly am not!" Janie replied indignantly. She did not know what a Ephorian was but by the tone of the mesmerizing creature's voice, she did not think she wanted to be one.

The creature seemed satisfied and motioned with a twinkly pink and yellow wand. The tall men released Janie.

She landed in a thump.

"Ouch," she looked up. "You didn't have to drop me," she said rubbing her bottom.

The fairy-like creature circled her again. Janie straightened her pajamas.

"I am Princess Julia," the fairy spoke at last. "I am the twin daughter of the great King of Fluberbia."

Julia paused – as if waiting. Janie remembered her manners. "I'm Janie," she said looking around. "Where am I?"

"You don't know?" Julia asked, her curiosity sparked. Perhaps she is the one, the fairy thought, careful not to get too excited at the prospect. "This is Fluberbia!" she said waving her arms around, "and that is my home."

She stepped aside, and for the first time, Janie noticed the most exquisite and enormous castle she had ever seen sitting high atop a hill behind the fairy. The sun was rising in the background and its edges seemed to glow.

"Wow," Janie exclaimed. "So, like, you're a fairy princess?"

"I prefer the term aeronautically gifted princess," Julia said.

"Okaaay, aeronautically gifted princess. Interesting, but more importantly, does that wand do magic?" Janie asked.

"It does."

"Then do you think you can use it to get me back home?" Janie inquired. Her stomach was churning. Zia would be so worried and Janie didn't like being in strange places all alone.

"In theory," Julia said slowly.

"How 'bout in reality?" Janie felt the butterflies in her stomach turn to giant bats.

"It is kind of broken," Julia said.

"Can you get it fixed?" Janie asked practically. "Do people do that here?"

"It isn't that easy," Julia said.

"Figures," Janie sighed. "Story of my short life."

"It is more cursed than broken," Julia responded sadly.

"Well, that's a bummer," Janie said.

"It is indeed," Julia said. "See, I was born a twin and the Empress Ephora, my great-aunt, was forced to bestow her magical powers on me, through this wand but also with a special wink of the eye. My parents thought the magic of each, the eye and the wand, could work alone. Separately."

"Something tells me they your parents were wrong," Janie said.

"To the extreme. We discovered the powers were not supposed to be separated – after it was too late," Julia, tired of fluttering, landed. "My parents only wanted it to be fair. Claire didn't get any magic at all. They didn't know trying to give her some of mine would be breaking the rules."

"There are rules about who can have magic?" Janie asked, somewhat surprised.

"I'll say. And the number one rule here – is the oldest twin gets the magic. Claire is, and must always remain, only a princess."

"You make that sound like a bad thing," Janie said, confused as to why being a princess of any kind would be bad.

"My parents got this idea that my sister Claire and I could share the magic," Julia rolled her eyes. "Being the King and Queen and all, they sort of thought they were above the rules, so they made me give Claire the wand. I had the nose twitch, after all. They thought she could use the wand power and I could use my other powers."

"In your parent's defense, it does make sense."

"It was horrible. The skies opened up and crashed with explosive light for ten days. These horrible wings grew out of my back and our parents were taken by Ephora's flying zebras to a tower on the highest peak of Ne'r'goup Mountain."

"That seems harsh," Janie said, almost forgetting her own problem.

"It seems Ephora was just waiting for us to break a rule. Her goal is to seize Fluberbia. That was almost a year ago."

"So did she seize it?" Janie asked.

"Nope. Claire and I have managed to fend her off, even without our parents around."

"Holy cow! Without your parents! Who takes care of you and your sister?" Janie asked, knowing how frightened and sad she would be without her parents. Janie guessed this princess was not older than seven or eight. How can seven-year-olds live without parents? she thought.

"We take care of each other, with the help of Jim and Jack of course." Julia nodded to the two giants who Janie, er met, upon her arrival.

Janie looked over at the men and her anxiety relaxed a bit. "If they are just in a tower, can't they be rescued?"

"In theory," Julia used that word again and Janie realized it was probably not that easy or they would be free by now.

"There's that word again," Janie said uncomfortably.

"The highest peak of Ne'r'goup Mountain is surrounded by a lake of smoldering snot, the smoldering snot is surrounded by the Enchanted Forest and the forest is guarded by an enormous Cinderbeast, maybe beasts, plural. We are not sure. There is only one road up the hill and the only one to have ever been to the peak and return is my great aunt, the Empress Ephora. So in theory, yes, but in practice..."

Janie fought back her tears. She was sad for the princesses to be without parents, but she suddenly realized that she may be without parents as well. For all she knew there was no way back home.

"But..." Julia began again.

"But! But is good," Janie's hopes returned a bit. "Tell me about but."

"Just how did you get here?" Princess Julia held her breath waiting for the answer. She dared not believe it so, at least not until she heard the words.

"I'm not really sure," Janie began. "I couldn't sleep so I got up and this light from outside caught my eye. I couldn't tell what it was, so I went outside, across the street and up to this old building and there was this flower, this beautiful purple violet. It filled the air with the most wonderful violet smell and I had to get more. I bent down to get a bigger whiff. I felt car sick and the next thing I know, your buddies here are picking me, not so gently, off the ground." She looked at the big guys beside her.

"Sorry," one said.

"You can't be too careful," added the other.

"You fell through the flower!" Princess Julia breathed more than spoke. Then she got on her knees in front of Janie. "We have been waiting for you."

The fairy bowed deeply.

"I what?" Janie moved towards Princess Julia. "Will you please stand up and tell me what you are talking about when you say I fell through the flower; because that's just a little odd and more than slightly impossible."

Julia rose slowly, now in awe of Janie. She never thought 'the one' would actually come. To tell the truth, she wasn't even sure 'the one' really existed or if it was just a story told by the elders to keep the younger generation hopeful.

"You fell through the flower! Literally. Bent down to smell and swoop – here you are. You are the one. The one who can help Claire rescue our parents!"

Janie took a step backwards. "I think you have me mistaken for someone with a whole different set of skills," she said. "I'm supposed to make gingerbread houses tomorrow and my family will be worried when they find out I'm not in my bed. My Zia is going to flip."

"But the legend of the forest says you are the one. The one of the beguiling and magical flower. You are the only one who can safely lead Claire past the Ogre, through the forest and over the deadly snot."

"Deadly!?" Janie gulped. "Snot sounds gross enough, but deadly. I'm not crossing anyone's snot. Double true if it's deadly!"

The winged princess just ignored her. "You have come!" Julia leapt at Janie, took her in her arms and jumped up and down excitedly. "Besides," she finally said, "it is the only way you can get home."

Janie and Princess Julia — CCSS RL 3.3

Is Janie or Princess Julia more like your best friend? _____

What characteristics make _____ more like your best friend?

_____

_____

_____

Are you more like Janie or Princess Julia? _____

Why: _____

_____

Choose a character from *Fluberbia* so far and Compare and Contrast her character traits to yours.

Character _____   Both   You

Name: _____ Date: _____ #: _____

Constructed Response Comprehension

1. What makes Princess Julia special? _____
_____
_____
_____

2. Describe what happened to Princess Julia's parents? _____
_____
_____
_____

3. Analyze what happened in this chapter? _____
_____
_____
_____
_____
_____
_____

4. Princess Julia mentions her twin. Predict what you think Princess
Julia's twin will be like. _____
_____
_____
_____

Making an inference is as simple as reading between the lines. It is the same as drawing a conclusion based on what you have read, mixed in with a little common sense.

Inference = what you read + common sense

You make inferences all of the time. Say you are in a car and you hear a loud crash and glass shattering. You didn't see what happened but you can guess, or infer, that there was a car crash of some kind.

When you read, you make inferences about plot and setting and characters all of the time.

Use the graphic organizer to make inferences about

Character or Event:	
Janie falls through a violet and lands in another world...**FLUBERBia**	
Details from the Story:	**My Experiences:**
In Chapter 2, Janie lands with a thump in Fluberbia. Two giants pick her up and a fairy appears.	Giants and fairies are imaginary and it is impossible to fall though a flower and land in another world
What I can infer: I can infer that *Fluberbia* is going to be a fantasy and that all sorts of strange things are likely to happen.	

Name: _____ Date: _____ #: _____

Down to *Fluberbia* Active Reading: Making Inferences: CCSS.RL 1

Your Turn: Select an event or character from Chapter 2 and make inferences about what will happen later in the story.

Character or Event:

Details from the Story:

My Experiences:

What I can infer:

Name: _____**Date:** _____

Storyboard Your Narrative

Make up a story about you landing in Fluberbia and meeting Princess Julia.

Storyboard First

Frame One	Frame Two
_____ _____ _____	_____ _____ _____
Frame Three:	**Frame Four:**
_____ _____ _____	_____ _____ _____

Grade 03 Mathematics Performance Task 2
Fluberbia: Down to Fluberbia

MAT.03.CR.3.000OA.D.234 C1 T1

Grade:	03
Claim(s):	**Claim 1: Concepts and Procedures** Students can explain and apply mathematical concepts and carry out mathematical procedures with precision and fluency
Assessment Target(s):	1 D: Solve problems involving the four operations and identify and explain patterns in arithmetic
Content Domain:	Operations and Algebraic Thinking
Standard(s):	3.OA.8, 3.OA.5, 3. NBT.3
Mathematical Practice(s):	1, 2, 6
DOK:	2
Item Type:	CR (Constructed Response)
Score Points:	1
Difficulty:	Medium
Key:	40 = (10 x 2 x 2)
Stimulus/Source:	

Grade 03 Mathematics Performance Task 3
Fluberbia: Down to Fluberbia

MAT.03.CR.3.000NBT.D.212 Claim 2

Grade:	03
Claim:	**Claim 1: Concepts and Procedures** Students can solve a range of well-posed problems in pure and applied mathematics, making productive use of knowledge and problem-solving strategies
Secondary Claim(s):	Claim 2: Concepts and Procedures Students can explain and apply mathematical concepts and carry out mathematical procedures with precision and fluency
Assessment Target(s):	2D: Identify important quantities in a practical situation and map their relationships (e.g., using diagrams, two-way tables, graphs, flowcharts or formulas). 1 E: Use place value understanding and properties of operations to perform multi-digit arithmetic
Content Domain:	Number and Operations in Base Ten
Standard(s):	3.NBT.2
Mathematical Practice(s):	1, 2, 6
DOK:	2
Item Type:	CR (Constructed Response)
Score Points:	2
Difficulty:	Medium
Key:	See Key
Stimulus/Source:	

Grade 03 Mathematics Performance Task 3
Fluberbia: **Down to Fluberbia**

MAT.03.CR.3.000NBT.D.212 Claim 2

Princess Julia, Janie and the two giants must walk 953 yards to the great palace of Fluberbia. Fill in the chart to show the amounts of hundreds, tens and ones in the number 953.

Number	Hundreds	Tens	Ones
953	9	5	3

In the space below, write a number that meets the following conditions.
- The number must be between 1 and 9.
- When the number is subtracted from 953, the digit in the ones place of the difference is greater than the ones place of 953.

	9	5	3

4, 5, 6, 7, 8 or 9

Scoring Rubric: Responses to this item will receive 0-2 points based on the following:
2 points: The student demonstrates thorough understanding of subtracting numbers using place value by naming each place value correctly in the chart and writing the number in the ones place of the difference that is greater than 3.
1 point: The student demonstrates a partial understanding of subtracting numbers using place value by either naming each value of 953 correctly in the chart of by writing the number in the ones place of the difference that is greater than 3.
0 points: The student demonstrates inconsistent or no understanding place value and of subtracting numbers using place value and place value when solving multi-digit arithmetic

Grade 03 Mathematics Performance Task 2
Fluberbia: Down to Fluberbia

MAT.03.CR.3.000OA.D.234 C1 T1

> Princess Julia explained that the Ne'r'goup Mountains are surrounded by a lake of smoldering snot and the smoldering snot is surrounded by a forest. In this forest live the Cinderbeasts. The princess does not know how many Cinderbeasts there are, but she guesses that there are at least 10.
>
> Each of the 10 Cinderbeasts has 2 paws, with razor sharp claws, for hands and 2 more paws, with razor sharp claws, for feet.
>
> What is the total number of clawed paws the Cinderbeasts have?

Grade 03 Mathematics Performance Task 3
Fluberbia: Down to Fluberbia

MAT.03.CR.3.000NBT.D.212 Claim 2

> Princess Julia, Janie and the two giants must walk 953 yards to the great palace of Fluberbia. Fill in the chart to show the amounts of hundreds, tens and ones in the number 953.
>
> | Number | Hundreds | Tens | Ones |
> |--------|----------|------|------|
> | 953 | | | |
>
> In the space below, write a number that meets the following conditions.
> - The number must be between 1 and 9.
>
> - When the number is subtracted from 953, the digit in the ones place of the difference is greater than the ones place of 953.

Chapter 3: The Only Way Home

"The only way I can get home? This is insane," Janie said.

She moved away from the fairy and began rubbing her head.

"What's the matter?" Julia asked.

"I'm searching for a bump, or a lump or some other injury that could cause me to fall into a deep, deep sleep and dream up this whole thing. Maybe if I find it, I'll wake up."

"I am afraid you are not asleep Janie. You are very much awake, so welcome to the Kingdom of Fluberbia. It's fate, don't you see? Your destiny is to save us."

Julia took her hand and began pulling the older girl along a flowered covered path that suddenly opened up before them.

The flowers were beautiful, all violets in every shade of pink and purple imaginable. Janie gasped at their brilliance.

"We have to go tell Claire and prepare you for your journey," Julia said excitedly.

"Is it really my only way home?" Janie asked.

"And my only way back to being human, with a touch of magic, and the only hope for my sister and I to be normal again," Julia replied.

"But what if I'm not the one?" Janie asked.

"There's one way to find out," Julia said but did not tell her what that one way was. "Come on. Let's go find Claire."

Janie followed the aeronautically gifted princess, a bit reluctantly, unsure of this journey she was about to embark upon and more than a little uneasy about what would happen next.

CCSS RL. 3.3

Conflict in literature is the struggle that appears.

Specifically for Janie:

What is Janie's goal? _____
_____
_____
_____
_____

What must Janie overcome?
_____
_____
_____
_____
_____

What struggle appears here?

_____
_____
_____
_____
_____

Your thoughts so far...
_____
_____
_____
_____
_____

Chapter 4: The Violet Path

The Grand Palace of Fluberbia was spectacular beyond any fairytale castle Janie had ever seen or read about. Its golden guild gleamed in the Fluberbian sunshine.

The Palace was nestled high upon a hill and it took much longer to climb the winding road leading to the massive drawbridge than Janie thought it would by just looking.

The palace was so large it just looked closer. Objects in the mirror are farther than they appear, Janie thought to herself, only she was sure it read closer on her dad's car mirror back home.

Janie stopped when they reached what she hopefully assumed was the halfway point and looked back down the path they'd traveled, but it was gone.

She looked ahead and could only see the flowered carpeting on which they were walking about a half a mile ahead of her.

"What's with the path?" she asked Julia.

The beautiful path of violets came and went. It was there and then it wasn't. The flowers seemed to bloom just for them to walk upon and then disappear.

"Security. It only opens for people who are light of heart. It knows who is good and who is evil. It helps to keep bad people out of the castle. In theory anyway."

"You sure do like that word," Janie smiled for the first time since she arrived. "Good and bad. Almost like Santa's naughty and nice list."

"Who?" Julia asked.

"Wow, this is so a different world!" Janie said. "Never mind. Are we getting closer?"

"A few more miles."

The castle was triangular and perfectly symmetrical, with a layout ideal for warding off invaders. Unless the invaders come in the form of a magical and angry empress who steals your parents because they try to treat you fairly, Janie thought.

The curtain walls, or outside walls, were two thick, doubling back on themselves and forming not one but two shiny golden layers of protection.

"But gold's soft," said Janie in more of a question than a statement. "How does it stop bullets and cannons and things like that?"

"The gold is on the outside, the inside is made of a special metal, invented by my father, out of fiber and light. Nothing can get through it."

"It's absolutely beautiful," Janie said, truly in awe.

At each of the triangular points was a tower and the front point had two towers. Each tower had a lovely porch with jewel-encrusted awnings.

The fortress literally glistened. Its pink and purple walls, with gold gilding, shined up into the sky, causing the illusion of a halo hovering over the entire structure.

"Those porches don't look so very secure," Janie pointed out matter-of-factly.

"We don't really have any invaders. Not since Empress Ephora kidnapped my parents. There used to be great armies that came to challenge our family's right to rule the kingdom. Now, everyone is so afraid of the Empress, and the spell she's cast upon us, they don't come near. Did I mention the Empress is my great aunt and she sort of divided the kingdom?" Julia leaned in and whispered to Janie. "Besides, I think they like the way my sister rules. She is nice and treats everyone the same – fairly you know? She may have stumbled on to the secret of good government."

"We're just now studying government at my school. I don't know much about it."

"Near as we can tell, it is all about being respectful and nice even when you do not feel like it."

Janie shrugged. "Probably especially when you don't feel like it."

"We learned that you have to take people's money to give them the things they need: police, hospitals, roads, but my sister is really good at not taking too much and letting people figure things out on their own. If you give people the chance they usually try to do the right thing. Well, mostly anyway. She also worked with the people and passed a Fluberbian Declaration of Citizen Rights."

"We have a Bill of Rights – protects our freedoms and stuff," Janie added.

"Yep, that's what ours does. I hope my father listens to her when we free him."

The bats took a lap around Janie's stomach. We *have* to free him, she thought, because I need to get home!

"We live mostly in the front two towers," Julia pointed up the hill. "See, the bridge between the two?"

Janie nodded.

"It's a heated pool with a slide and a diving board."

"Cool," Janie said, noticing how hot it was here in Fluberbia and how a good swim would make her feel better.

"We are pretty modern here, television, the Extranet..."

"Extranet?" Janie asked. "What is the Extranet?"

"Well, it is really what you call your Internet," Julia said. "See, my father is a brilliant engineer and he figured out a way to harness the signals of other worlds. We can watch earth's television, tap into the Internet and even download movies. We call it the Extranet – because it really is just full of extra things to do. You know when the important things like reading and playing and going to school, are done. We also get signals from Globia, Miopa and Flannet, but they do not have reality TV like you all do. I love my reality TV."

"Whoa," Janie was surprised.

Janie watched the road before her unfold in a symphony of flowers.

The smell of violets was intoxicating and made her almost forget where she was and that there was a good possibility she would never ever actually see home ever again.

She looked behind her, and just as quickly as they appeared, they were gone. The flowers that made the path faded into the dirt as if they never existed.

It made Janie sad. What if that was going to happen to her? What if, by falling into the flower, she just faded off into the dirt and was gone and nobody on earth would ever remember she existed?

"Janie? Janie? We're here," Julia nudged her back to present.

Name: _____   Date: _____

Comprehension Questions for Critical Thinking: *"The Violet Path"*

Answer the following questions using complete sentences.

1. What is special about the violet path?
2. Describe the castle.
3. What did Ephora do to the princesses' parents?
4. Why do you think they liked each other? Or -- Why do you think they did not like each other?
5. What do the princesses do with people's money?
6. What modern things do they have in Fluberbia?

Name: _____   Date: _____

The Violet Path

Please correct the mistakes in the sentences below. Remember to look for punctuation, capitals and misspelled words.

1. "Whats wit the path?" she asked julia.
Corrections:
2. princes Julia walkd easily a long the Path?
Corrections:
3. Janie & julia both goed to the beautiful Palace
Corrections:
4. The girl walked to gether as the flours opened befour them
Corrections:
5.   Thee palace was bigg pink and Gold. janie thout it was pretty?
Corrections:

Name: _____ Date: _____ #: _____

Dictionary Skills

Look up the following words and write the definitions below.

Word	Definition
empress	
fiber	
illusion	
hover	
invent	

Scan back through the story and write down any words, so far, that you are unsure of. Look up their definitions and write them below

Word	Definition

Grade 03 Mathematics Performance Task 4
Fluberbia: The Violet Path
MAT.03.ER.3.000 NF

Grade:	03
Claim:	**Claim 1: Communicating Reasoning** Students can clearly and precisely construct viable arguments to support their own reasoning and to critique the reasoning of others
Secondary Claim(s):	**Claim 2: Concepts and Procedures** Students can explain and apply mathematical concepts and carry out mathematical procedures with precision and fluency
Assessment Target(s):	3 B: Construct, autonomously, chains of reasoning that will justify or refute propositions or conjectures. 1 F: Develop understanding of fractions as numbers. 1 K. Reason with shapes and their attributes
Content Domain:	Number and Operations – Fractions
Secondary Content Domain:	Geometry
Standard(s):	3.NF.3, 3.G.2
Mathematical Practice(s):	3, 6
DOK:	2
Item Type:	ER (Extended Response)
Score Points:	2
Difficulty:	Medium
Key:	See Sample

Answer Key

Sample Top-Score Response:
Part A: 1/5
Part B: 1/5

Part C: The areas are different. Rectangle M and Rectangle N are now the same whole. The sizes of the areas are different. The shaded areas are different. The area of Rectangle N is greater than the area of Rectangle M.

2 points: The student demonstrates partial understanding of explaining fractions as number and reasoning with shapes and their attributes to support his or her reasoning by expressing the area of the shaded region of Rectangle M and Rectangle M each as 1/5 of the area of the given rectangle and then by giving a complete explanation of why the shaded areas of the two rectangles are not equal.

1 point: The student demonstrates partial understanding of explaining fractions as numbers and reasoning with shapes and their attributes to support their own reasoning by expressing the area of the shaded region of the Rectangles each as 1/5 the area of the given rectangle and then by giving a partial or incomplete explanation about why the shaded areas of the two rectangles are not equal.

0 points: The student shows little or no understanding of either concept.

Grade 03 Mathematics Performance Task 4
Fluberbia: **The Violet Path**
MAT.03.ER.3.000 NF

Part A: Rectangle M is divided into 5 equal parts. Each part represents a violet on the path to the great Fluberbian Palace.

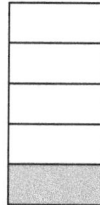

Rectangle M
What fraction is represented by the shaded area of Rectangle M?

Part B: Rectangle N is divided into 5 equal areas, as shown.

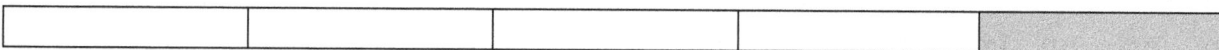

Rectangle N
What fraction is represented by the shaded area of Rectangle N?

Part C: Is the shaded area of Rectangle M equal to the shaded area of Rectangle G. Explain your thinking. Use what you know about the area of Rectangle M and Rectangle N to explain

Read and Think:

Chapter 5: The Princess Claire

Before them expanded lush green grass and a grand drawbridge. Surrounding the palace was a sparkling blue mote with dolphins playing in the crystal clear water.

"We replaced the sharks when the invasions stopped," Julia said as they crossed the mote.

"Awesome!" Janie replied, meaning it.

"Besides, Ephora's the only one we really want to keep out and she loved the sharks. Come on."

Julia led Janie into an enormous hall. The floors were covered in pink marble and the railings, up the grand staircase, was more golden than the gilding on the walls.

"It's twenty-four caret," Julia said. "Welcome to our home."

"Wow," was all Janie could say as they wound up the left side of the stairs.

Resting on columns, at the top and bottom of each side of the stairway, were apples of pure clear polished rubies that glistened in the natural light, casting the sun's glow from the palace's many windows and skylights and scattering it throughout the room.

Janie stopped when a figure appeared at the top of the striking staircase. It was a young girl, with flowing golden hair, slightly darker than the railing, clear blue eyes and the sweetest smile Janie had ever seen.

> **Use Your Own Words to Describe the Palace**
> _____
> _____
> _____
> _____
> _____
> _____
> _____
> _____
> _____
> _____

The other princess was dressed in an azure gown that matched her eyes. Janie thought to herself that if she was ever to imagine a princess, she would look just like Claire.

"That's my sister," Julia said, using her wings to flit up to the other girl. "Janie I would like you to meet Princess Claire."

Claire extended her hand and Janie didn't know whether to shake it or curtsey. So she did both.

"Hi," Claire said. She looked at her sister. "You are not supposed to go out without telling me," she scolded.

Julia ignored the reprimand and leaned in. "She is the one," she whispered.

Claire's eyes lit up. "For real?" she asked her sister.

"For real," Julia answered.

"She came through the flower?" Claire asked.

"She came through the flower," Julia confirmed. "And," Julia continued, "the path opens up for her as well."

"Like us?" Claire asked, astounded.

"Just like," Julia said.

"You must be hungry," Claire said to Janie, and for the first time, Janie realized she was indeed hungry, very hungry. "Take her to the kitchen and give her breakfast while I go change. We have a long journey ahead of us."

Without a word Julia led Janie out the back and down a different, but equally grand, staircase to the kitchen.

A large stone fireplace lined an entire wall and a kettle bubbled and brewed over it. The whole place amazed Janie. It was a contradiction – a mixture of things that didn't match or make sense.

Large television screens lined the parlor she'd just been in as well as the walls in the kitchen. Blaring into the somewhat medieval room was a show about a bunch of college kids sharing a house.

Reality TV for the cooks, Janie thought. Yet, she did not see a stove, just two large fireplaces and an old-fashioned trash burner. She knew what a trash burner was because her Zia had one.

"Hallo," called a portly woman, without looking from the television.

"We are going to get breakfast," Julia said.

"You sit right down," another woman, with a large bun on the top of her head, said. "And I'll bring it right to you."

The woman with the bun dipped a large ladle into the pot over the fire and Janie was sure she saw something crawl into it. She raised her eyebrows as the cook put the bowl down in front of her. It was some sort of mush or gruel and it seemed alive, crawling with large jellyfish like objects.

"It's moving," Janie said, without realizing she was using her outside voice.

"Those are the dophrines. They are a delicacy," Julia said as she slurped up her own.

"Perhaps just some toast," the cook said placing dry toasted bread in front of Janie. "Butter?" she asked.

"Yes, please," Janie answered politely.

The cook placed a dish in front of her and the butter seemed just as alive as the mush.

Janie ate her toast dry and was finishing up as Claire entered the room, this time dressed in shorts, boots and what looked to Janie to be a shirt right out of Robin Hood.

Janie wiped her mouth. "Do you two have a plan or are we just going to wander around until we find your folks and hope a key is dangling from where they are locked?" asked Janie.

"The plan is to go through the forest, over the snot, up the mountain and rescue my parents," Claire said matter-of-factly.

"Oh, silly me," Janie said somewhat sarcastically, "I was afraid you hadn't thought it through."

"You are the one," Julia said confidently. She could just feel it was so.

"So, you say. Only I have no idea what that means or what I am supposed to do. Being the one and all," Janie said.

"This is going to be a grand adventure!" Claire said. "And hopefully we will get our parents back."

"Maybe Janie is right. Have you thought about how you are going to get through the forest and over the snot and up the mountain? And what about the parchment?"

"Parchment?" Janie parroted.

"I almost forgot," Claire said.

"Miloph is keeping it," Julia said. "He has the instructions..."

"...and the test," Claire finished her sister's sentence.

"Yes, the test," Julia remembered.

"Test?" Janie asked. She didn't like tests so very much.

"To make sure you really are the one," Claire said.

"I thought you said you were sure I am the one," Janie said growing more uneasy by the second.

"We should hurry," was Claire's answer as she led the girls out of the kitchen, down a long spectacular hallway and back to the front foyer.

"Before Miloph goes up to his perch for the day." Julia opened the grand wooden doors to let the warm sunshine stream in.

"Wait!" Claire said suddenly and everyone stopped. "Janie's in her pajamas."

Janie totally forgot. She looked down. She was in pajamas, purple Scottie dog pajamas and a pair of floppy pink Uggs. The Fluberbian air was so warm she'd forgotten she didn't have real clothes on.

Claire grabbed her hand and the two girls raced up the stairs and found clothes for Janie. They were back inside of ten minutes. They left the castle together with the two giants, Jim and Jack, trailing behind them. Janie noted how these two men seemed to follow the princesses everywhere they went.

Fluberbian Food

Describe the food you eat:

Describe Fluberbian food:

Pretend you are a chef at the Grand Fluberbian Palace. Plan an exotic and ALIVE menu and write it below! The crazier the better!

Grand Palace Menu

Name: _____ Date: _____ #: _____

Comprehension Questions for Critical Thinking: "The Princess Claire"

Answer the following questions using complete sentences.

1. What was resting on the columns and at the top of the staircase?

2. What confused Janie about the kitchen?

3. Describe Fluberbian butter.

4. What does Claire state as the plan?

5. Claire grabs Janie's hand. Where does she take her?

6. Who has the parchment?

Chapter 6: Miloph

This time, when they crossed the drawbridge, Janie noticed a village to the south of them. It was quaint, with wooden structures brightly painted – alpine style. The village was in what appeared to be a valley with a rushing river running through its center.

All around were statuesque mountains. The tallest was ominous, scary, with a hazy cloud hovering at its base. Janie guessed this would be the one they had to conquer.

Miloph, it turned out, was a large blue bird with orange eyes. He reminded Janie of the tiny blue bird from her game that, when touched, flashed into three birds.

When Miloph saw the girls approaching, he swooped off of a large, bejeweled nest and spoke with a whistle. "Princesses!" he called happily, "so nice of you to vissssit your old friend."

Janie should have been surprised to hear a bird speak, but nothing about Fluberbia surprised her and she'd only been there a few hours.

How could it surprise her, she thought. How could anything ever surprise her again? One minute she was safe and secure at her Zia's and the next she fell through a flower...a flower! And was scooped up by two giants.

Then she met a fairy princess with a twin, who is a princess without the fairy part, and now she was going to climb a mountain and risk her life to save their parents, all to get back home again.

Actually, she liked the princesses and felt sorry for them. There was a loneliness about them she felt compelled to fix. Janie was young, twelve to be exact, but she was an old soul and a fixer. If she saw someone in need, or felt that someone was sad, she would try to make it better. It was her nature.

"And who is thissss?" Miloph buzzed Janie and landed in the center of the three girls.

"She is the one," Julia said.

Miloph preened his feathers.

"Or at least we think she is the one," Claire corrected her twin.

"I see," Miloph said skeptically circling Janie. When their parents were first taken, many claimed to be the one, only Miloph would send them away. For the real *one* had to enter through the magical violet and solve the riddle of the first gem. None of the others did or could.

Miloph sniffed the air. This one smells right, he thought.

"She came through the violet," Julia said. "I saw. I was out when I wasn't supposed to be, so it is fate."

"The violet you say?" Miloph let down his brow, "interesting..."

"Give her the test Miloph! Please!" Claire said excitedly.

"Then we can get our parents back," Julia added.

"Girls, I fear it is not that simple. For even if she passes the test, the journey to your parents is rife with many a danger and there is no guarantee of success," Miloph warned.

"But she's the one," Julia answered. "You always said if the one came through the violet, she would be able to read the parchment and rescue our parents."

"Read the parchment, I said. Go after your parents, I said. She is the only one who may be able to conquer the path that Ephora has laid out," Miloph cautioned and Janie felt like she was going to be sick. Her head was swirling and she could taste her breakfast again – which wasn't a good thing -- because, it wasn't all that tasty the first time around.

"So blonde one," Miloph began.

"Janie," Janie gave the funny bird her name.

"Janie," Miloph called her by name, he was a polite bird after all. "Are you ready for the test...for the riddle?"

Janie swallowed and slowly nodded.

"All right then," Miloph flew back up to the bejeweled nest high above the ground and quickly came back with a small scroll. He dramatically cleared his throat and began,

"Sugar and pots
or gloriously shot,
ones they are cooked –
ones that do rot.
Scrumptiously golden,
brown, orange, red and green...

over the top now

they're not what they seem.

Newton's top

and teachers' hop.

One and now the doctor stops.

Figure it out...

find it for fact...

protect you it well

to there and to back."

"That's it?" Princess Claire asked.

"That's all I have," Miloph said.

"But what about the parchment?" Julia asked.

A parchment was just a piece of paper, but the kingdom had been told, during Ephora's mighty tirade, the one in which she took the princesses' parents, that Miloph would be left with the secret of the parchment and therein would lie the secret of their rescue.

"I assume solving the riddle will bring about the location of the parchment," Miloph said as he handed the scroll containing the words of the riddle to Janie.

"Good luck," he added as he flew back up to his nest.

"Wait," Janie called and the bird swooped back down, "is that really all you know?" she asked.

"Well..." Miloph hesitated.

"Come on Miloph," Julia began.

"Please tell us everything," Claire finished.

Miloph cleared his throat and leaned towards the girls. He spoke in a low voice. "The journey will be difficult and once the riddle is solved you will be presented with the empty crown of the Kingdom of Ephora. This will come in a vision and, as you collect the gems, the crown will become whole."

"The crown grandfather spoke of before he died?" Julia asked.

"The Crown of Goodness?" Claire added.

"Children, your parents were taken, because they tried to separate the magic bestowed upon the first twin of your generation, by the Empress herself. She gave the magic in exchange for the gems of goodness that once encrusted her crown and made her good. It was all part of a deal your grandfather, the fourth King of the Kingdom Fluberbia, made with his sister Ephora."

"Wasn't she supposed to get the crown after their parents died?" Claire asked.

"Indeed, but sssshe didn't," Miloph said. "They gave it to your grandfather instead – with the condition he was to give it back in exchange for keeping Fluberbia whole. They knew Ephora was waiting to split the kingdom. Ephora refusssssed and a great war broke out and the kingdom was divided and ravaged."

"Then why did she part with the magic?" Claire asked.

"She had to. She had to grant her brother's first born grandchild the magic of the family – if of courrsssseee that grandchild was a twin – or she would be cursed."

"So this is a family fight?" Janie asked.

"That it is. Your grandfather was so furioussss when Ephora broke up the kingdom – he sssssssssscattered the gems of goodness beyond the four corners of Fluberbia – emptying the crown and enraging his sister."

"But then he didn't have the gems when he needed them," said Claire. "I get it."

"Yes, in exchange for the magic, your parents promised the gems, only he could not get them without help from the one beyond the flower," the bird said.

"Janie," Claire said.

"Your parents did not know that Julia could only summon Janie with all of the magic together. The magic they split it up."

"So, by splitting it between us, the only thing we could do was wait," Julia said.

"Exactly. When the magic was split, you lost your power Julia and the direct line to Janie."

"But she came anyway," said Julia.

"Indeed she may have. We knew she would eventually," said Miloph.

"But why did Ephora take our parents?" Julia asked.

"Ephora was furioussss and a pure evil fell upon her. If she can't have the gemsssss, she intends to conquer Fluberbia and needed your parents out of the way. She can't help it for it is part of the curssssssse."

"But we don't have the gems," Claire said logically.

"But you do," Miloph said, only none of the girls knew exactly what he meant.

"Where does the flower come in?" Janie asked.

"There is a legend, that a great savior from a world beyond, will come to Fluberbia, through the mystical violet, but only when the conditions are right and only when the kingdoms needs her most," he explained. "That time is now and the ressssscue will be beyond just the king and the queen, but that is not for now."

"The peace won't last?" Julia asked.

"Peace is a precariousssss thing and you may not be able to withstand the power of Ephora – even without the magic, she is stronger than you know. She is plotting againsssst you assss we ssspeak."

"But when she has the gems – can't she just attack us anyway," Claire asked what the other girls where thinking.

"The gems have a magic of their own and those who possssessss them asss a ssset sssee only goodness and act only with kindness."

"Cool magic," Janie said, knowing the trouble in her own world.

"So if we find the gems and return them to the crown – she turns nice and we save Fluberbia," Julia said.

"And I get to go home," Janie sighed.

"Can we take Julia on our, uh, adventure and use the magic to help us?" Claire asked.

"I can only imagine how much help we are going to need," Janie said, frightened about the journey ahead, but a little excited about the adventure.

She couldn't help but think about her brother and how much she could use his help in figuring all of this out.

"The twitch and the wand were designed to work together. They would be usssselesss to you. Besssides, one of you must stay here. For if both of you parish before there is an heir, the whole of Fluberbia will fall into the hands of Ephora and we will all be doomed," Miloph said sadly. "And then there issss the magic. It must be reunited or..."

"Doom again?" Janie interrupted.

"Exactly, my dear child," the bird said.

"Why?" Claire asked what they were all thinking.

"Because the magic is what keeps the sssun and the ssstars in the sssky," he looked up.

The girls looked up as well.

"They do look droopy," Julia noted, fluttering above the pine trees for a closer look and then swooping down and putting something into Claire's pocket without anyone noticing her doing so.

"Indeed they do," said Miloph. "Indeed they do."

"So what do we do specifically?" Claire asked.

"The journey to your parents will lead you to the gemsss, each in sssuccession after you solve its riddle. Once these gems are returned to the crown, Ephora's darkness will vanish, the wand and the twitch will rejoin and the prison tower will disappear. Then and only then will your parents be free."

"And, of course," Claire added, "Fluberbia will be saved."

"There issss that as well," Miloph said.

"Sounds easy," Janie said, using that sarcastic voice again, "piece of cake."

Of course, when she looked over at the princesses, she was sorry for the tone she used. They needed her and she needed to get home. She looked down at the scroll containing the riddle.

"The journey through the Forest of Gaul will take you to the edge of Gulch of Doom," Miloph continued.

"Let me guess, full of real Ogres?" Janie asked.

"Of the most frightening sort," Claire answered, in a tone that made Janie shiver. She'd never met an Ogre she liked. They frightened her.

"The Prince of the Ogres has the emerald hidden. The hiding place is revealed in another riddle. The next gem, the sssapphire, is somewhere deep within the Enchanted Forest. You will have to find and solve the riddle leading to its location as well."

"And the next?" Janie asked almost afraid to know.

"The diamond. At the mouth of the great Snot Pit of Ne'r'goup Mountain. It is large and glistening and will stop the flow of snot, enabling you to cross to the bassse of the mountain upon which the tower was built."

"But weren't there four jewels?" Julia asked – vaguely remembering pictures she'd seen of Ephora's crown.

"Yes," Claire added, "what about the ruby?"

"Indeed," Miloph said, as he scratched his beak with his right wing. "Indeed there wasss a ruby."

"Wait," Janie unrolled the scroll and re-read the riddle.

"Sugar and pots

or gloriously shot,

ones they are cooked –

ones that do rot.

Scrumptiously golden,

brown, orange, red and green...

over the top now

they're not what they seem.

Newton's top

and teachers' hop.

One and now the doctor stops.

Figure it out...

find it for fact...

protect you it well

to there and to back."

"So?" Claire said, not understanding what the riddle had to do with the ruby.

But Janie was already off, sprinting back to the castle. "Come on," she called to the others, but did not slow down or look back.

Claire ran to catch up – while her feathered friend and fairy sister flew in front of her.

Janie raced over the drawbridge, pulled open the massive doors and sprang at the staircase as the others, breathlessly, entered the palace to see her touching the first of the apple decorations adorning the banister.

"Of course," Claire cried joining her.

"Green and red and yellow, Newton. Teachers. The doctor will stop. Apples!" Janie cried triumphantly.

"Of course!" Julia joined them.

"The ruby was here all along." Janie touched the last red apple and it literally sprang to life, casting fiery sparks throughout the great hall entryway. It jumped from her hand, or appeared to so much as gems can jump, and spun in place, hovering in the air.

Once, twice it spun, until a tiny scroll, like that containing the riddle, fell to the ground.

"Holy cow," said Julia.

Claire ran to the parchment. She retracted as she touched it. "It shocked me."

Julia reached for it next and was thrown against the banister. "Ouch!"

"Janie you try," Miloph said.

Comprehension Questions for Critical Thinking: *"Miloph"*

Answer the following questions using complete sentences.

1. What is Miloph?
2. What is the parchment?
3. What does the parchment instruct the girls to do?
4. Recap: Who is running Fluberbia?
5. What do the Ogres have to do with the story?
6. How will they make Ephora's darkness vanish?

Miloph

GOAL: To gain a better understanding of the story through reading and writing.

Directions for Classroom Use: Cut the sentence strips and assemble them into a complete paragraph.

They learned that the princesses' grandfather scattered gems intended for Ephora to the four corners of the kingdom and that the gems could only be recovered with the help from the one beyond the flower.
Miloph, it turned out, was a large blue bird with orange eyes. He reminded Janie of the tiny blue bird from her game that, when touched, flashed into three birds.
Janie came through the violet, so Miloph read them all the parchment.
Janie figured out that the first gem was one of the rubies that decorated the palace.
Miloph told the girls that he assumed solving the first riddle will help them find the second.

Activity: Socratic Discussion/Seminar

Common Core Anchor Standards Addressed: R1, R2, R5, W1, W9, SL1 and SL4
Teacher Page: Socratic Discussion/Seminar

A Socratic Seminar is a structured discussion that allows students to engage and disagree in a way that is polite, focused and respectful. This activity enables students to think critically about texts and build confidence in their ideas and thought processes. The discussions that take place within the Socratic Seminar help students analyze, synthesize and evaluate the written word.

Students begin a Socratic Seminar with a list of teacher (or student – depending on the level) generated questions that help the group think critically about the text they are reading. Students pose questions to the group and take turns speaking and listening to each other's thoughts and ideas. Learning is shared by all members of the discussion as students work together to gain a deeper understanding of text as they extend, challenge and clarify themselves and each other.

Before you begin, develop a signal to politely stop any student who may be dominating the conversation.

1: Students should complete an **Investigative Clarifier** (Titled "Seminar Template") to gain a deeper understanding of the text.

2: Guide each student to complete the Seminar Template directly following this section. This can be done in class or completed as homework.

3: Break into groups – or circle up one group with leftover students acting as scribes.

4: Establish the rules and norms of the discussion.

5: Review the purpose of the Socratic Seminar and your expectations. Model how students should participate and behave.

6: Select a discussion leader.

7: Set time limit – 30 to 40 minutes is sufficient.

8: Begin the discussion.

9: Debrief – include discussing the group's strengths and weaknesses.

Helpful hints: If your class is large, divide students into two circles – one inner and one outer. Leave one chair in the inner circle empty. This is the "roving seat". Students who are in the inner circle are active discussion members. Students in the outer circle can pop in! If it is not the first time you are doing this activity – you can actually have two Seminars going at the same time. Twenty is about the limit for active participation for all; however, students are more engaged if the student participation rate is closer to twelve.

It is imperative to stress that students must reference the text often and that thinking out of the box and analyzing out of the box are essential, and encouraged, for this activity. Teachers should stay out of the conversation, but guide if necessary.

Name: _____

Socratic Seminar Template One: <u>Fluberbia</u>

Discussion Question:

Janie has a magic power that will help her help the princesses find their parents.

Site two main ideas or claims from the novel to support your argument as it relates to the question.

1.	2.
_____ _____ _____ _____ _____ _____ _____ page	_____ _____ _____ _____ _____ _____ _____ page
List examples SUPPORTING your argument: _____ _____ _____ _____ _____ _____ _____ _____	List examples COUNTERING your arguments: _____ _____ _____ _____ _____ _____ _____ _____

Name: _____

Socratic Seminar Template: <u>Fluberbia</u>

Discussion Question:

There is evidence that Fluberbia is a magical place. Pose both arguments.

Site two main ideas or claims from the novel to support your argument as it relates to the question.

1.	2.
_____	_____
_____	_____
_____	_____
_____	_____
_____	_____
_____	_____
_____ page	_____ page
List examples SUPPORTING your argument:	List examples COUNTERING your arguments:
_____	_____
_____	_____
_____	_____
_____	_____
_____	_____
_____	_____
_____	_____

Chapter 7: The Journey Begins

Cautiously and slowly, Janie reached for the parchment. She touched it and felt nothing. She was able to grab hold and unravel the delicate paper. "It's a map," she said almost to herself.

The palace quaked, as thunder clashed and lightening flashed away the ruby. An eerie silence replaced the rumble and Ephora's head appeared before them in a ghostly hue. The empty crown rested regally on the suspended head...empty except for the ruby now securely in place.

In an instance, the vision was gone.

"One down," Julia said, trying to sound enthusiastic.

Janie and Claire looked at the map. It was moving.

"Whoa," Janie said, "it's alive."

Claire giggled. "Of course it is. All maps in Fluberbia are interactive."

A tiny screen popped above the picture of the castle and appeared to blow in an imaginary breeze.

Claire squinted at the picture as words appeared. "Another riddle."

Janie leaned it and read it aloud:

"Green as the grass
and tucked safely within,
the house of the grouse
and the big blue tail fin.
The forest for trees,
the Ogre despise,
the tallest of these
right between the two eyes.
Gulch but to cross
for Ogre to see.
Walk a day's time
and there we will be."

> **Predict...What is the Riddle Solution?**

"So we're going to the forest," Janie said and they were off.

Fluberbia, So Far...In my Opinion

What is your favorite part of the story?
Details why...
1.
2.
3.

Who is your favorite character in the story?
Details why...
1.
2.
3.

What is the main problem in the story so far?
Details...
1.
2.
3.

What is the solution to the problem?
Details...
1.
2.
3.

Summary 4-Panel

Summarize this chapter in four pictures.

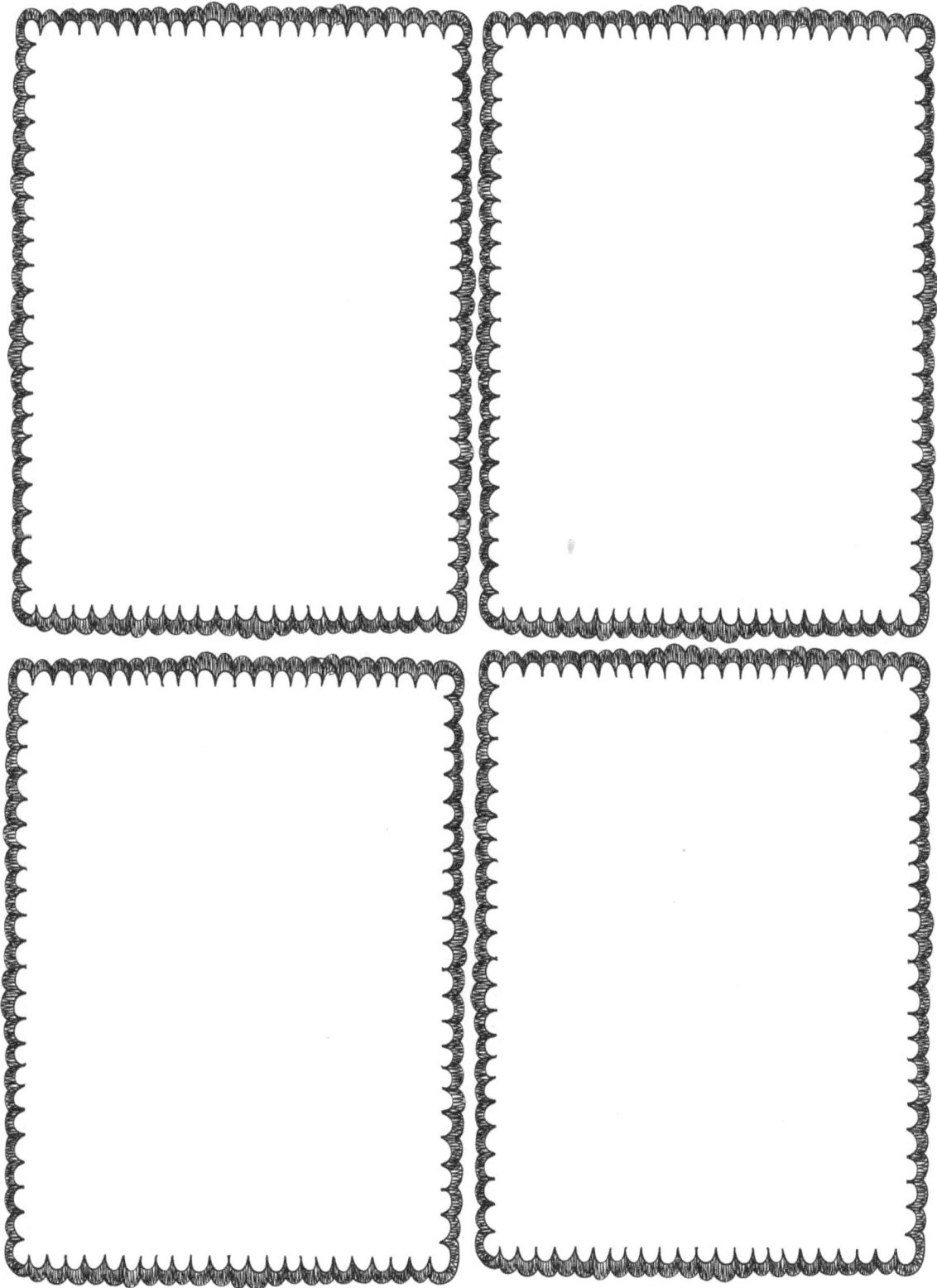

Constructed Response Comprehension Questions for Critical Thinking

The Journey Begins

1. What happened when Janie touched the parchment? _____

_____

_____

2. What was on the parchment? _____

_____

_____

3. What happened after the palace quaked? _____

_____

_____

_____

4. What is special about the map? _____

_____

_____

_____

Close Reading

Read 1:

Circle the words that will help you summarize this chapter.
Underline anything that jumps out at you.

Chapter 8: Flash

The violet path stretched before Claire and Janie, but only so far as the next ten steps.

Janie looked at the map and shuttered to herself – startled – having forgotten it was alive – so to speak.

"So the violets will take us to the forest, if we follow the map?" Janie asked.

"I think the violets only go as far as the edge of Fluberbia and then we're on our own," Claire said.

"Have you ever been to the forest?" Janie asked – breathing in a big whiff of the dainty violet smell. The soft scent made her feel good, as if everything would somehow be okay. Eventually.

"I've never been outside of Fluberbia," she said and they walked in silence for a long while.

The trees in Fluberbia were numerous shades of brilliant green, bright and alive as their leaves blew in the breeze and the sky was the deepest blue Janie had ever seen.

When they reached the border of the Kingdom of Fluberbia, but not near to the forest yet, Claire stopped.

"This is as far as I've ever gone," she looked back at the castle and the village, both tiny in the distance now. "Janie I'm a little frightened," she said softly.

"I'm scared out of my mind!" Janie exclaimed enthusiastically. "This whole thing is too scary for words," she put her arm around the younger girl, "but we don't really have a choice here."

Claire took a deep breath and nodded.

"And we are together. That makes us tough."

"It does?" Claire asked.

"Sure it does," Janie said, not really so certain herself, but wanting to make the smaller and younger girl feel better. "Besides," she said pointing at the road before them, "in front looks the same as behind."

Claire closely examined in front and then did the same to behind and she felt a bit better. "I guess you are right."

"Course I am. Besides, you rock! You've been living alone without your folks for months and you've survived that."

"Oh Janie, I miss them so much. I could never have done it without Julia with me."

Janie nodded and took the step to beyond Fluberbia. She sighed because she missed her family and couldn't imagine how Claire must be feeling having been without hers for so long. She said a little prayer to herself that she would one day find her way home.

Beyond Fluberbia looked very much like inside Fluberbia...with its rolling hills, beautiful trees and dense wildflowers.

The path was not violets now, but made of crushed pink stone. There were neat fences on either side of them. When they passed the occasional home – painted pink – for pink was the color of

The text says:

_____
_____
_____
_____
_____

I already know:

_____
_____
_____
_____
_____

So, I can infer:

_____
_____
_____
_____
_____
_____
_____
_____

the beyond – the people stopped and stared, some even whispered.

The girls caught words here and there. Most about the princess and the stranger and the speculation of a rescue.

The pink houses had dome roofs made of grass now.

"You ever read The Wonderful Wizard of Oz?" Janie asked.

"I am afraid I have never heard of it. Why?" Claire asked as they walked farther and farther from Fluberbia.

"Just wondering. This place reminds me of Dorothy walking to Oz before she meets the scarecrow only everything is pink here and was blue there."

"So not very much the same at all," was all Claire said.

They walked until they spotted an apple tree. Claire looked at her cell phone. "It's lunch time," she said.

"You like apples?" Janie asked.

"You bet I do," Claire answered as she climbed the tree and started gently tossing fresh crisp red apples to Janie. "I like 'um green better, but I'm starving," she said, simultaneously sliding down the trunk and taking a bite the a juicy apple.

Janie pulled out the map and pointed to where it was literally blinking *you are here*.

"We're almost there," Claire said. She started to say something else, but stopped and began staring at something in the distance.

"What?" asked Janie looking in the same direction, trying to figure out what caught her new friend's eye.

"The bushes are moving," Claire whispered softly.

"Everything here moves," Janie said matching her tone.

"No," Claire pointed to a corner, "something is in them."

Janie looked from her perch on a tree stump. "They're berry bushes, maybe something is stuck."

Claire moved beside Janie and carefully the girls approached the bushes. They both jumped back when the green leaves and red berries began to shake and quake.

"Holy cow!" Claire said as she moved closer.

"Wait," Janie reached out to grab Claire's arm but was not fast enough. "Claire!" she said nervously as the bushes rocked again.

"Look!" Claire carefully parted the prickly bushes to reveal a horse as white as the puffs of clouds floating overhead. "He's caught."

The horse looked at the girls and whinnied sadly.

"You think we can free him?" Janie asked as she saw the horse was tangled not only in the bushes but in the remains of an old fence as well.

"Here," Claire said as she petted the horse's nose and gently began untangling the wire.

Janie went to work on the bushes and in no time the horse was free and standing on all fours.

Claire pulled out a napkin she had in her pocket and dipped it into the babbling brook. She carefully cleaned the horse's wounds. The horse was so grateful it nudged happily against her.

The horse stepped back and seemed to bow to the girls.

They giggled and petted his nose and then he bowed lower – as if he was beckoning them to get on.

"You think he wants to take us to the forest?" Claire asked.

"We'd get there faster if we rode," Janie said.

"And it's probably safer to have him with us," Claire added as they climbed on the grand stallion's back and Janie used his mane to carefully guide them in the direction the map indicated was the forest.

After they traveled a bit, the scenery began to change. The foliage grew thicker and a canopy of trees overtook the sunshine until it was fully swallowed up above them.

"Janie?" Claire spoke as they galloped steadily through the forest.

"Yes," Janie answered.

"Do you think we should name him?" Claire asked.

"Great idea," Janie patted the horse's head and he looked up at them and they both thought he smiled. "What do you think we should call him?"

"Hummm," Claire thought, "What about Flash because he is so fast."

Janie patted the horse's head again. "What do you think boy? Do you like Flash? Huh boy?"

The horse whinnied his approval.

As the sun set fully behind the distant volcanic mountains, the girls noticed the first pink house with a thatched roof they'd seen in a long time. Behind the house was a yellow barn. Janie coaxed Flash to a stop.

"It's getting dark," Claire noted.

Janie took out the map and reread the riddle aloud:

"Green as the grass
and tucked safely within,
the house of the grouse –
the big blue tail fin.
The forest for trees, the Ogre despise,
the tallest of these,
right between the two eyes.
Gulch but to cross,
for Ogre to see,
walk a day's time
and there we will be."

"It has been a day's time," Claire said, "almost exactly."

"But we galloped. I wonder how long it would have taken us to walk?" Janie thought out loud.

"Who do you think lives there?" Claire asked.

"The houses are the same as the ones in Fluberbia. Could it be one of you?" Janie asked hopefully.

"No Fluberbians come this far," Claire said.

"You think it's an Ogre?" Janie asked.

"I've always heard they lived under the ground in the Gulch of Doom."

The text says:

_____
_____
_____
_____
_____

I already know:

_____
_____
_____
_____

So, I can infer:

_____
_____
_____
_____
_____
_____
_____

Janie located the Gulch of Doom on the map. It was beyond the River Blear. "It doesn't look far."

A rattle from the direction of the house caught the girls' attention.

"What was that?" Claire asked.

"Sounded like someone opened a door, but no one is there."

"Janie?"

"Yeah?"

"I don't want to stay in the forest at night. I'm not so big on the dark."

"I didn't really think about that," Janie looked around at the dusk turning to night, "until now."

Read 3

Things I find confusing:

Things I find interesting:

Things I connect with:

Things I can connect to my life:

Chapter 9: The Stranger

"You think we should see who lives in this house?"

Before Claire had the words all the way spoken, the door opened again and out walked a tiny man.

"Hallo, hallo," called the stranger.

Janie grabbed Claire's hand protectively. "Stay close to me and don't let him separate us."

Claire squeezed Janie's hand. "Janie," she said tugging at the older girl, "whatever happens, thank you for this."

The man waddled to them. "Young and girls. White horse. In the forest. Forest at dark. Why?" He spoke funny and emphasized the wrong words, but the girls understood what he meant.

"I am Claire, Princess of Fluberbia," Claire said regally and stood in front of Janie.

"Ah yes," the little man moved closer and squinted up at Claire's face. "The twin ruler. Rule twin. Absent parents."

"This is Janie," Claire introduced her friend.

The little man sniffed the air around Janie. "I see. See I." His eyes twinkled. "You are she. Not you are?"

"What do you mean?" Claire said.

"Nothing, nothing," he said as an owl hooted and the girls jumped. "Come along. Flash, too. Barn. Put him in the barn. We eat," the man said as he headed back towards his front gate.

The girls followed, but Janie stopped, pulling Claire back. "Wait! How did you know the horse's name is Flash?"

Claire stopped short. Yes, she thought, how did he know. They never told him the name.

"Many things. I know many things," he held the gate open for them. "Along you come."

The girls looked around.

"Do you think it's safe?" Janie asked, her heart beating so fast she felt it echo through the forest.

"I don't know," Claire whispered, "but I think we will find out."

They followed the little man into the barn where he led Flash. He fluffed up some fresh alfalfa and patted the horse down before he wordlessly headed into the typical Fluberbian house - way out of Fluberbia.

He showed the girls to a tiny table by a stone fireplace. "Hungry?" he asked.

"No thank you," Claire said politely, but her rumbling stomach gave her away.

"Ogre I am not," the man said – reading their minds, "but I know their journey."

"How did you know Flash's name and that we are looking for the Ogres?" Claire asked what Janie was thinking.

"I am Goloph. Cousin to your father," he wagged his finger at Claire, "and your kin as well," he wagged the same finger at Janie.

Janie looked at Claire and they both raised their eyebrows.

"You must have me confused with someone else," Janie said. "I came..."

"Through the flower," the little man finished her sentence. "You are the one. The one. Or you'd be there. There you are not, because here you are."

The man lifted the lid of a cauldron hanging over the open fire. The smell of fresh stew wafted through the air. He scooped out three bowls and set them on the table, one in front of each girl and one in front of himself. "Eat," he said digging into his dinner. "Long day. Tomorrow, long day for you both."

"But...cousin? Kin of Janie's? How? Who are you?" Claire asked as she politely ate the thick brown food in front of her.

"That is not now. Eat and then sleep. Long day. Long day indeed," Goloph finished his stew, picked up all three bowls, even though the girls' were not yet finished, scrapped the food into a sink and put the dishes into a dishwasher.

Janie noticed the irony of a dishwasher but no stove. She didn't have a chance to ask about that or further what Claire wanted to know, what she wanted to know, her Uncle? How could that be? She was Janie from earth and she wanted to go home. The little man pointed out two small beds in the corner and then disappeared behind another tiny door, leaving the girls gaping behind him.

"What just happened?" Janie asked as they stretched out on the beds that were more akin to cots.

"Funny little man," Claire said.

"Do you think we are safe?" Janie asked.

"I feel safe, but he is not Fluberbian."

"You think he is an Ogre?" Janie asked.

"Do you think he is related to both of us?" Claire asked.

"Do you think we are related?" Janie asked hopefully, for that would mean she was part princess or something like that anyway.

"Before my grandfather died, he told Julia and me stories of the magical violet and of our family on the other side. I think, my new friend, there is more to you and me than we yet know."

Janie smiled and yawned. "I think you're right."

"I know you miss home, but I'm glad you came."

Janie smiled at the littler girl. "Me too."

"I hope we are related," Claire said.

"I can't wait to hear the story," Janie said. "I bet it is a hum-dinger."

"I'm really sleepy," Claire yawned.

"Let's sleep in shifts. "You go first," Janie said, but they both drifted instantly into dreams.

Claire and Janie woke to the sun shining in the windows. The house was empty. It was odd they woke at the same time, rubbed their eyes and got up for the door, again at the same time.

Flash was waiting for them in the barn, rested, fed and ready to go.

"I wonder where Goloph is?" Claire looked around as they readied to leave. "I wanted to thank him."

A flutter of dirt swarmed up the walk. "Girls," Goloph called, "some food." He handed them a basket. "To the king. Good wishes. Wishes good," he said.

"Who are you Goloph?" Claire asked softly as she hugged him for his kindness.

"Banished long ago," he shook his head, "mistakes to right with you."

The girls climbed on Flash's back.

"What does that mean?" Claire called as they began to gallop away.

"You will know my children. Know you will," he called and Janie realized the little man looked a bit like her father and Zia and a bit like herself.

"Do you think we will ever know who he is?" Janie asked.

"Someday we will know everything my new friend," Claire said. "I just feel it."

Name: _____ Date: _____ #: _____

chapter summary – Fluberbia

Answer the questions for the chapter titled: "The Stranger"

character(s)	
setting(s)	
plot – problem	
plot – solution	

How does this chapter help move the story forward? please be specific.

_____

_____

_____

_____

_____

_____

_____

_____

_____

_____

_____

_____

_____

Character Study: Janie

Action: What did she do?

Character Traits

Janie

Motivation: What did she do it?

Name: _____ Date: _____ #: _____

Dictionary Skills - Fluberbia So Far

Look up the following words and write the definitions below.

Word	Definition
ominous	
scary	
caution	
protective	
invent	

Scan back through the story and write down any words, so far, that you are unsure of. Look up their definitions and write them below

Word	Definition

Chapter 10: The River Accident

They rode Flash to the edge of a great rushing River Blear.

Janie pulled out the map. "We have to cross."

"How?" Claire looked up and down the river for a narrow spot or a place where the water wasn't rushing quite so swiftly.

They were watching the water and did not notice they'd walked into a swarm of bees.

Flash tried to brush the buzzing bugs away with his tail. He lurched forward to get away from them. They were so thick, he couldn't see. He stumbled over the river rocks. He lost his balance and they all went soaring into the raging water.

The girls screamed as they hit the rough, cold water and struggled to hold on.

Flash tried gallantly to avoid the rocks over which the water splashed. His muscles ached under the pressure of the girls struggling to hold on.

"Don't let go," Janie yelled as Claire's grip loosened.

"I'm trying," Claire called as the water splashed up into her face again and again.

Just then, Janie lost her grip and the girls tumbled off the struggling horse. Janie swallowed a gulp of water and went under.

Flash frantically swam towards her and nudged her to an open sandy spot along the shore. Janie coughed and sputtered as she looked down the river for Claire.

The other girl was bobbing through the churning water, swiftly approaching a waterfall set high above a turn in the river!

"Claire!" Janie screamed but could not be heard over the roar of the water.

Flash looked from one girl to the other, as if he knew, as if he sensed he was her only way to safety. He ran down the length of the shoreline. Janie followed.

Claire had stopped precariously close to the waterfall and was holding on to a rock, but she was losing her grip.

"It's slippy!" she screamed.

"Hold on Claire, please!" Janie yelled as she looked around for something long enough to toss out.

"I can't!" Claire cried.

Flash reared and nudged Janie to the water. He turned around and held his tail out.

"What boy?" Janie asked. "What are you saying?"

"Hurry!" Claire called desperately.

"You want me to hold on and go in?" Janie's eyes were wide. "I still don't think I can reach. Oh! Wait! I can use your tail as a rope. Is that what you mean?"

Flash patted his paw on the beach once and nodded his long head. Janie held her breath, tied the horse's wet tail to her foot and carefully walked into the water as the horse backed up.

Janie struggled to keep her head above the water. It was churning between her and the rock, but not so much as beyond – not so much as where Claire was.

Flash stopped when the water reached his belly – as if he knew going farther in would cause him to lose balance again, only this time they would all tumble over the falls.

Janie was fully in the water now, extending her body and free arm as far as she could. "I can't reach!" she said. "You have to let go with one hand."

"I can't!" Claire yelled.

Flash cautiously took one more step towards the rock. Janie was so close.

"I'm slipping!" Claire said – panic setting in.

"You have to reach for me," Janie took another deep breath. "Seriously, on the count of three let go of the rock and dolphin dive to me."

"I'm scared," Claire said softly.

"Me too," Janie admitted, "but it is the only way."

"One," Janie said slowly but loudly, "two, three!"

Claire closed her eyes and dove towards Janie's hand. Janie reached as far as she could and grabbed it tightly. The weight of the extra girl tugged on Flash. He struggled to hold his footing. He was slipping deeper into the water, teetering to hold his balance.

"Come on boy!" Janie coaxed.

Flash stopped and took a step out of the water, then another and another, slowly pulling the girls behind him.

The girls hugged when they were safely on the shore. Then they ran to the horse and snuggled his neck and he seemed to snuggle back.

"You saved me," Princess Claire said and Janie noticed a regal tone.

Janie remembered her friend was a princess and was about to ask if the horse could be knighted for his bravery or something when the ground beneath them shook. They stopped and looked at each other. It happened again, this time more fiercely.

"The Ogres," Claire said in a hushed tone, but matter-of-factly.

"The Ogres?" Janie asked.

"Yes, we were told stories of the Ogres when we were younger so we would not wander out of Fluberbia. They are mean and magical and work in the mines. They are evil and tricky, but they are slow. Legend has it that twice a day, once when they go down into the mines and again when they come up, their great train causes the earth the tremble."

"Do you think they're going down or coming up?"

Claire looked at the sun in the sky and realized they must have gotten a really early start, as it was still morning. "I'd say going down, which is the perfect time for us to figure out how to get the emerald."

"We find it first," Janie pointed out.

"I always heard it was in the center of the Gulch of Doom," Claire said nervously. "Doesn't sound very inviting."

"It's the doom part that gets me," Janie whispered. "Yikes."

"But there will only be two Ogres out now. The guards. If of course the stories are true. And two is better than hundreds, right?"

"If you say so," Janie said and took another deep breath. She wondered why it was suddenly so difficult to breath in this strange world.

Comprehension Questions for Critical Thinking: The River Accident

1. Who fell in the water and how? _____

_____

_____

2. What does Claire say about the Ogres? _____

_____

_____

Summarize This Chapter in Pictures

Setting Studies: The River Accident

Book Setting	This Chapter Setting

Write the Definition of Setting:

Your Favorite Setting from this book	Create Your Own Setting for Fluberbia

Chapter 11: The Gulch of Doom

They reached the edge of the Gulch of Doom when the sun was high in the sky. Claire pulled out her cell phone and up popped a message for YP. She thought it odd her royal cell phone received such a text. She was regally blocked from spam, but this one felt different. This one she didn't want to erase.

The gulch was like a large desert – a canyon with high walls and no way up or down. It was barren and foreboding, except for a cluster of trees hiding the entrance to the underground Ogre dwellings. A large mineshaft stood at one end. Two large towers guarded the mines. The girls could not see Ogres in the towers but both instinctively knew they were there.

They dismounted Flash and moved back into the forest – where they felt protected from the sightline of the Ogre guards.

Janie pulled out the map and read the riddle aloud once more.

"Green as the grass and tucked safely within, the house of the grouse – the big blue tail fin. The forest for trees, the Ogre despise, the tallest of these, right between the two eyes. Gulch but to cross, for Ogre to see, walk a day's time and there we will be."

Claire stepped out of their cover of safety, but only a bit. "The only thing green down there are the trees covering the doors in the ground," she said.

"That's probably where they live," Janie joined her, nervous to be exposed out in the open. "And look at the sky...those clouds..."

"Oh my!" exclaimed Claire when she looked up to see the clouds part to reveal the blue sky in the shape of a big fish tail fin.

Claire pointed to the two tallest trees that seemed to form an arch near the top of the gulch and below the fin. "Those two trees, over there, forming the arch. They've got to be three hundred feet tall."

"The tallest of these," Janie repeated. "But what about the eyes?"

And then they saw it, at the same time, the outline of a person? Ogre? Something.

"Between the trees. It looks like and outline of Goloph," Claire said.

Sure enough, it did.

"You're right," Janie said. Wondering if they were wrong to trust him. Wondering if the Ogres now knew the girls were coming. "And look there." Janie pointed to the forehead of the outline and there, sparkling in the reddish rock of the gulch, was an emerald – polished and shiny.

"It's the emerald!" Claire exclaimed. "You know it is supposed to be the first taken from the Ogre's emerald mine and gifted to my great grandfather when there was peace between the Ogres and Fluberbia."

"Why isn't there peace now?" asked Janie.

"The most fertile part of Fluberbia used to belong to the Ogres, but we owned the water rights. One day they decided to stop paying for the water, so my grandfather dammed it up. A war broke out. The fighting lasted only a year, but there is still no real peace between them and us and we have lost most passage outside of our land. And they," Claire made a sweeping gesture over the gulch, "have very little water."

"Wow," Janie said. "Just like my world."

They were silent – staring at the gem in the rock.

"So, how do you suppose we get to it?" Claire asked.

"You got me," Janie said, "remember we have to get the gem and get across the gulch – under the watchful eye of those guards." She pointed to the towers.

Claire sunk down in the soft moss of the forest and leaned against Flash. "I'll never see my parents again," she said sadly, as if she already rendered the task too difficult, as if she had already given up.

Janie sat beside her. "You can't give up now."

"It all seems so hopeless," Claire sighed.

"Hopeless for you?" Janie asked. "You are my new hero."

"Hero? Me? I am just a frightened princess," Claire said, finally sounding like the little girl she actually was.

"Seriously? No way." Janie nudged the girl. "You are so brave. Your parents were stolen and you took over their kingdom! Talk about scary. Alone with your sister, without parents or experience and – from what Julia said – you are bringing peace to the land."

Claire shrugged. "Adults think too much," she said. "They'd figure it out if they just treated others the way they wanted others to treat them."

"You have that here too?" Janie asked.

"Yes, and it seems to get worse the older grown-ups get," Claire shook her head. "If we do rescue my parents..."

"When we rescue your parents," Janie interrupted.

"When," Claire managed a small smile, "we rescue my parents, I hope they understand how easily the peace can be broken and just be willing to compromise once in a while."

"Hopefully," Janie said.

Main Idea: The Gulch of Doom

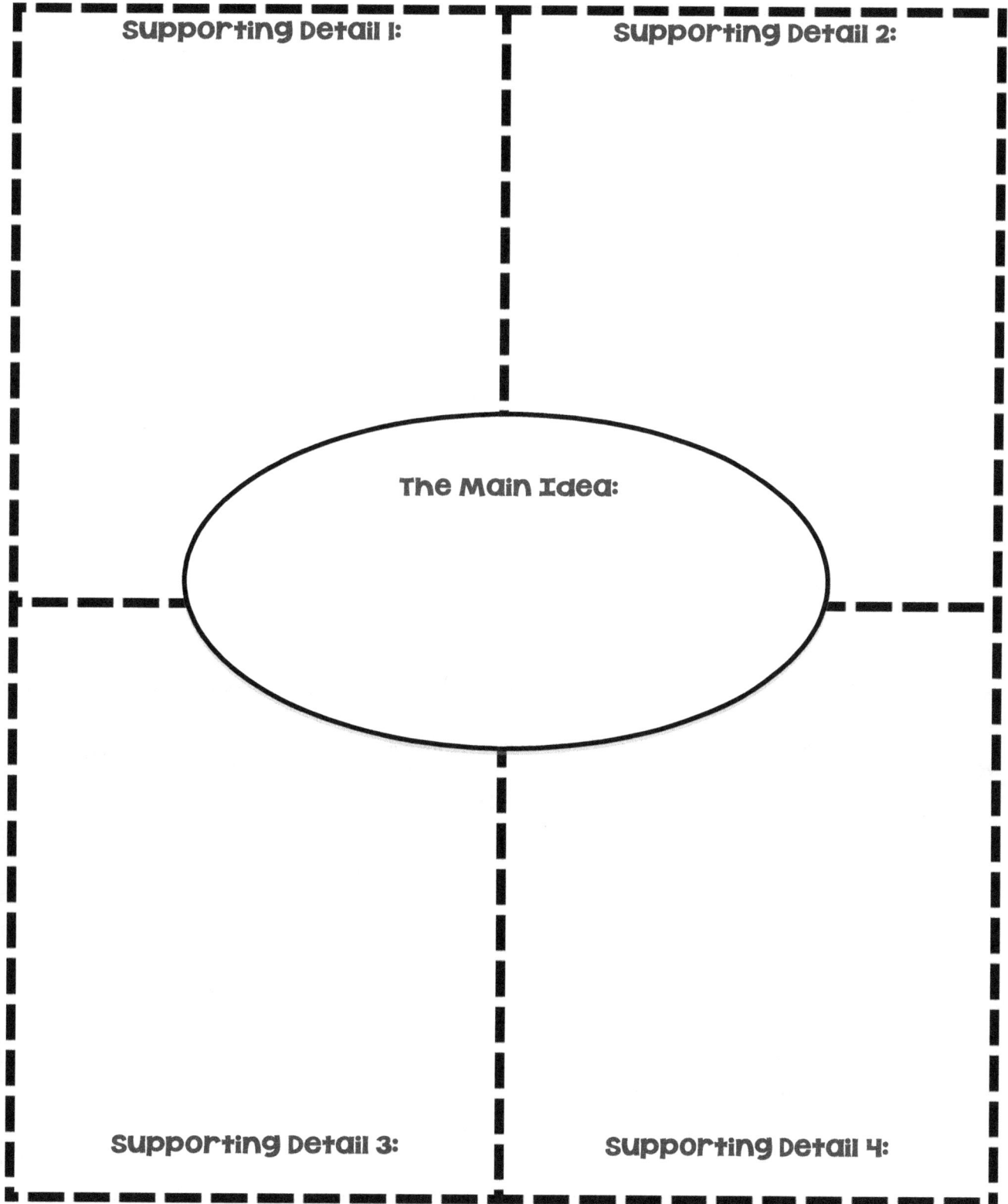

Supporting Detail 1:

Supporting Detail 2:

The Main Idea:

Supporting Detail 3:

Supporting Detail 4:

Name: _____ Date: _____ #: _____

From Dialogue to Character Traits

Select three quotes from the same character and write them below. Next, use the quotes to infer your character's character traits.

Super storytellers don't always come out and tell you every character detail...sometimes they imply them through dialogue!!

Quote:

Quote:

Quote:

Character: _____

What can you infer about your character from the quotes?

Name: _____ Date: _____ #: _____

Comprehension Questions for Critical Thinking: *"The Riving Accident"* and *"The Gulch of Doom"*

Answer the following questions using complete sentences.

1. What is Flash?
2. How did Flah save the girls?
3. What was odd about Claire's royal cell phone?
4. What does Claire comment is the only thing green in the Gulch?
5. Why does Janie tell Claire she is brave?
6. Claire tells Janie's that adults think too much. How?

Name: _____ Date: _____ #: _____

Character Study: _____

Action: What did she do?

Character Traits

Motivation: What did she do it?

Chapter 12: To the Bottom

They didn't realize how long they'd been sitting and staring into the gulch until the ground beneath them began to tremble again and they noticed the sun was sinking in the sky.

"They're coming up already," Janie said.

"Do we have a plan?" Claire asked.

Flash seemed to understand. He got up off the cool, comfy ground and walked to the edge of the gulch. He stared until the Ogres came out of the mine and marched, single file, to their homes. As darkness crept up around them, lights flashed in the guard towers.

"They don't leave," Claire said.

Janie squinted at the towers.

"Am I insane or does the guard in the far tower look like Goloph?" Janie asked.

Claire leaned towards the tower, but she was too far away to really to tell who it was with any certainty.

"Sort of, but Goloph isn't a Ogre or at least he doesn't really look like the ones I've dealt with since my father has been gone. He looks Ogreish, but not fully and he is nice. Ogres are terribly bad tempered and have a spiteful streak, even to their own kind," she said.

"You think they stay awake all night?" Janie asked.

"It appears so," Claire said.

It was dark enough for them to join Flash at the edge of the gulch. The light that slowly rotated in circles from the guard towers only served to illuminate small portions of the ground below at any given moment.

"If we time it right, we can use the darkness to shelter us," Claire said.

"I was thinking the same thing," Janie said, "it's just hard to tell how far it really is across the desert and if we can clear the open stretch without being discovered."

"Then there is the problem of getting to the bottom," Claire said, looking down the face of the gulch wall. "It is too steep to climb."

"We could really use your sister's wings," Janie said.

Claire nodded.

"We'll have to scale down the..." Janie began but stopped when Flash approached her and bent down for her to get on. "What is it boy?" she asked.

"I think he wants you to get on," Claire said.

Janie climbed on the horse. Flash walked to their right, to a space hidden by bushes. He walked through the bushes to reveal a path. "Claire, over here," Janie called, "there's a path."

Claire joined them and it was true, there was a path down. A very steep and narrow path but a path nonetheless.

Flash moved forward.

"Wait," Claire called, jumping behind Janie.

This seemed to aggravate Flash, but the girls pushed forward.

"Come on boy," Claire said. "Take us down."

The horse huffed and stomped, as if trying to tell them something.

"It's okay, Flash," Janie said. "Let's just hurry and get the emerald before morning."

Flash carefully walked down the steep path. It was barely wide enough for him to fit all four hooves upon it at the same time. Tromping on the very narrow parts caused the side of the gulch to give way, trickling rocks down the steep wall to land on the gulch floor.

Janie looked over the edge but quickly looked back straight ahead. Her heart was pounding outside her chest again.

Each time the path caved in down the gulch, Claire tightened her grasp on Janie's waist a bit more.

The deeper they ascended, the more at risk they were of being discovered by the guards in the towers and their slowly rotating lights.

It happened when they were almost at the bottom. The path narrowed too much for the horse to hold his footing, he stumbled and tried to regain his balance, but not before Claire tumbled off his back and over the edge of the cliff.

She frantically reached for the rock wall, scraping her fingers along the rough edges, finally grabbing hold of a jagged rock sticking out farther than the others.

Janie caught her breath as she watched her friend fall and was frantically relieved when Claire grabbed hold of the wall, until Janie realized she had no way of helping the other girl down.

Claire was stuck, hovering over the gulch, just waiting to be discovered.

Still atop Flash, Janie descended the remaining portion of the path to the bottom of the gulch, jumped off of the horse and ran to the spot over which Claire hung.

And then they were discovered. The light crossed their path and they froze and for a moment they thought they were okay, but then the light tracked back and held and an alarm sounded and they were caught.

Janie placed Flash under Claire. "Jump," she called up.

"I can't," said Claire, "I'm scared."

"You have to. They're coming," Janie coaxed.

Claire held her breath, closed her eyes and let go of the cliff.

She landed with a thump on the back of Flash. Flash jerked, but held Claire. Janie climbed back up and Flash was off towards the crux of the two trees.

Neither girl noticed the slight limp in Flash's gape as they speed towards the other side of the gulch.

The alarm was sounding louder now. Loud and long it wailed into the night and the doors of the homes began to open wide. Hoards of Ogres made their way towards the horse and its riders.

Janie and Claire held on tightly to Flash as he lowered his head and plowed into the Ogres on his way across the desert gulch.

A small man, Ogre-like, but not an ogre – caught Claire's eye.

"Look!" she pointed him out to Janie.

"Goloph!" Janie whispered, but quickly turned her attention back to the road.

It was Goloph indeed, walking towards them from the direction of the mine.

"Halt!" he called loudly and forcefully and the Ogres immediately stopped.

Flash kept running, full speed, towards the emerald.

The Ogres huddled around Goloph and a tussle broke out. Shouts and rustling echoed off the gulch walls and several Ogres broke free and ran slowly after Flash and the girls, who were now stopped between the trees.

They looked up at the emerald.

"Even if we get it out, how will we ever escape?" Claire asked.

"They're coming for us!" Janie said.

"The riddle! How do we get it?" Claire asked.

Janie took out the map and read: *"Green as the grass and tucked safely within, the house of the grouse – the big blue tail fin. The forest for trees, the Ogre despise, the tallest of these, right between the two eyes. Gulch but to cross, for Ogre to see, walk a day's time and there we will be,"* she stopped. "Grouse's house. What is a grouse?"

"Birds! Look!" Claire pointed up to a flock of giant grouse descending upon them, dive-bombing the Ogres. One stopped next to Flash and looked up at Claire.

"We've been waiting for you princessss. Hop on," he lisped.

Claire looked at Janie. Janie nodded her approval. They really didn't have a choice.

Claire gently climbed upon the bird's back and he took off towards the emerald.

"Welcome princesssssss..." he squeaked joyfully. "Watch the branchessss."

Claire ducked just in time to avoid crashing into a large branch.

"Nice reflexesss..." the grouse laughed. "I'm Popperas."

"I am Claire," the princess said politely.

"I know who you are. We've been waiting. Sent by your father." They were directly in front of the emerald. "Pull it quickly and close your eyes," he warned.

Claire followed his directions. When she pulled the emerald, the entire wall glowed a brilliant and fiery yellow. Silence spread over the gulch.

The emerald danced in Claire's hand. Ephora's head appeared again under the crown – this time the ruby and emerald glistened in the vision.

The Ogres were descending upon Flash and Janie. Popperas swept down and called to Janie.

"Hop on," he yelled.

"I can't leave Flash," she said.

"Flash is a creature of the forest. He is not an enemy of the Ogressss. He will find you again if there is ever the need," the bird lisped, "if it is his destiny."

Flash nudged Janie with a tear in his eye. She nuzzled his neck and reluctantly left his side.

"Thanks boy," she said and he nodded and they were off, soaring up and over the far side, one step closer to rescuing the king and queen.

Comprehension Questions for Critical Thinking: *"To the Bottom"*

Answer the following questions using complete sentences.

1. Who does the guard in the tower look like?

2. What could it mean if the "person" in the tower is who the girls' suspect?

3. How did the girls' get down the gulch?

4. What does this riddle reveal to the girls?

5. How does the grouse help Janie and Princess Claire?

6. Summarize "To the Bottom" in five sentences.

Name: _____ Date: _____ #: _____

Learn the Skill: Story Sequence

What is this skill? **Sequence** is the order in which things happen. As you read, think about what happens in the beginning, middle, and end of a story. You can also look for clue words and phrases that help you understand when things are happening.

Why is this important? Good readers need to pay attention to the sequence of events in a story. This helps them to keep track of what happens.

What happens at the beginning of this chapter "To the Bottom":

Beginning:

Middle:

End:

Chapter 13: The Enchanted Forest

Popperas flew them to the edge of the most beautiful forest the girls had ever seen. He landed in a bed of colorful pansies and the girls hopped off his back.

"Thanks Popperas! You saved the day," Claire said warmly.

"And quite possibly our lives," Janie said sincerely believing it true.

The bird bowed, so much as a bird could. "It was my pleasure princessss. Travel carefully through the foresssst and remember what is evident to the eyessss is not necessssssarily what is the truth."

Before they could ask what the grouse meant, he was gone.

Janie walked to the end of the pansy field and peered into the dark forest.

"It's so pretty," she said.

Claire followed and took a long, deep whiff. "And it smells positively heavenly."

Janie breathed in deeply. "Ummmm, it sure does." She sat down in the flowers and laid her head back. "So, that was scary."

Claire sat too, smiling, haggard but proud of what they did. "It was, but we did it."

"I'm going to collapse now, but we did!"

They both giggled proud of their accomplishment.

"I wonder if we will ever see Flash again?" Claire asked.

"I hope so, he's a good horse," Janie said sadly.

"And a good friend," Claire said.

"Don't you royal people have a medal for that?" Janie asked.

"If we see him again, we can probably work something out," Claire said, happy having known Flash, but sad to have left him behind.

Janie took out the map.

"One more time," Claire said.

The map blinked their new location and up popped their next riddle.

"As I suspected, this is the Enchanted Forest," Janie said.

"I could have told you that without even looking," Claire said. "Can't you tell this place in enchanted? Can't you feel it?"

Janie sort of nodded. "I suppose with all of the flowers and stuff."

Claire pointed to a tall peak still a distance behind the forest. "Look. That must be the highest peak of the Ne'r'goup Mountains, the one that's surrounded by a lake of smoldering snot and the smoldering snot is surrounded by an enchanted forest – this enchanted forest – and this enchanted forest is guarded by the enormous and ferocious Cinderbeasts. So, we should get going, find the sapphire and move on."

"Very practical," Janie said as she tugged the edges of the virtual map to make it bigger. The next riddle blurred and then came into focus. *"Golden yellow, blue and pink...something to eat, upon which to think. Open the door, built by no man, grill up the fire – rocks in the pan."*

"That makes no sense," Claire said.

"Not yet," Janie pointed to the map. "The golden path is blinking. Gold is the first color listed. I think we should try that direction."

"This forest is enchanted. Do you think it is a trap?" Claire asked.

"I guess we'll find out," Janie said, getting up and pulling Claire with her.

They walked into the forest and stayed on the golden path. They marveled at the walls of enormous flowers with stems as large as tree trucks and gigantic blooms that shaded the midday sky.

The colors were brilliant and the flowers grew in every shade of the rainbow.

They came to a tunnel of delicate pink, white and yellow roses. It was dark inside and the smell wafted out to the path.

"It's dark in there," Claire said, not particularly fond of the dark.

"It is the only way through to the blue path," Janie pointed to the map again. "See? The path turns blue about halfway through."

They looked at each other, held hands, took a deep breath and began through the tunnel.

About halfway to the other side, they heard a strange humming coming from not so far in front of them.

"What do you suppose that is?" Claire asked.

"I was about to ask you the same thing. This is your world remember," Janie said.

"I fear this is as far from my world as it is from yours my new friend," Claire said.

They stopped and stared ahead as they noticed something was glowing in the distance.

"A light," Janie said. She looked down at her feet and clicked her heels three times.

"What are you doing?" Claire asked.

"Just hoping," she said wistfully. "If I get home I am going to figure out a way to get you The Wonderful Wizard of Oz to read."

Claire didn't understand all Janie wished for, at that very moment, was a pair of magical shoes to get her home.

As they started and progressed on their journey, Janie couldn't help but wonder if she, like Dorothy from Kansas, had the power to get home buried deep inside her.

They started to walk again. The silence of the darkness now broken, Claire spoke as they headed towards the humming. "Do you think Goloph was friend or foe?"

"Good question. I wondered if you saw him too." Janie said.

"I do not think we have seen the last of him," Claire said.

"I bet you're right," Janie said, more quietly than before, as they were now upon the buzz. "It's a sword!" Janie said.

"In a rock," Claire said, "how odd."

"I assume it is there because we're going to need it," Janie said moving to the sword and tugging on it.

"It looks like it is in that rock awfully deep. You'll never get it out."

"Excalibur!" Janie exclaimed.

"Ex – what – i - bur?" Claire asked.

"Excalibur. The sword in the stone, King Arthur, the legend of Excalibur?" Janie said.

Claire shook her head, not understanding the reference.

"This place is one allusion after the next," Janie sighed.

"What's an allusion?"

"We are so alike, but the differences are in our references. Everyone in my world would get what I mean – Dorothy, Excalibur – but you don't. Interesting," Janie said.

"I suppose," Claire sounded a bit confused.

"Excalibur was a special sword cast into a stone. It could only be removed by the true and rightful king of England, which is a country in my world. You are a royal. The daughter of a king. I bet you can pull this thing right out of that big rock," Janie said.

"You are a bit older and stronger than I. If you couldn't do it, how do you suppose I will be able to?" Claire asked earnestly.

"Because you just will. It isn't about strength. It's about the right to use the sword," Janie said. "Try and see."

Claire slowly approached the humming sword and looked back at Janie.

Janie nodded to her. "Try," was all she said.

Claire looked back to the sword in its own stone, put both hands on the handle and tugged up so hard, she and the sword went tumbling backwards into Janie. Both girls feel to the ground.

Light illuminated the cavern of roses. The sword gleamed in its own glow.

Claire smiled despite herself. "Cool," she said.

"Way cool," Janie said, standing and helping Claire and the heavy sword up with her. "Will you be able to carry it out?" Janie asked, noting how heavy it was.

"It looks heavy, but it isn't," Claire said, handing it to Janie to test. The golden sword fell to the ground.

"Must be you. It is way heavy for me," Janie forged ahead. "Guess you'll be carrying it alright," she laughed.

Claire smiled proudly – happy to do so.

Comprehension Questions for Critical Thinking: *"The Enchanted Forest"*

Answer the following questions using complete sentences.

1. Why is this chapter called "The Enchanted Forest"?
2. What is the name mountains in the distance that Princess Claire pointed out?
3. What is the significance of the tall peak in the distance Princess Claire pointed out?
4. Describe what happens with the sword?
5. What could Princess Claire do that Janie could not?
6. Summarize "The Enchanted Forest" in five sentences.

The Enchanted Forest

GOAL: To gain a better understanding of the story through reading and writing.

Directions for Classroom Use: Cut the sentence strips and assemble them into a complete paragraph.

As they headed deeper into the forest, Janie began to wonder if she would even get home again.
Princess Claire and Janie found a sword in a big rock.
Popperas flew them to the edge of the most beautiful forest the girls had ever seen.
The sword was too heavy for Janie to carry, but it was no trouble at all for Princess Claire.
Claire pointed to a tall peak still a distance behind the forest. "Look. That must be the highest peak of the Ne'r'goup Mountains.

The Enchanted Forest: Fix it Up

Please correct the mistakes in the sentences below. Remember to look for punctuation, capitals and misspelled words.

Princs claire and janie walkd thru the Forest?
Corrections:

JaniE wondered, if She would ever get hom again
Corrections:

princes Claire foud a Sword in a larg rok.
Corrections:

The enchanged Forest was fulled with trees
Corrections:

Chapter 14: The Cinderbeast

Claire smiled as she walked – proud to carry the special sword. For the first time, the loneliness in her heart she felt for her parents lessened. For the first time, she believed they really did have a chance of rescuing them.

The blue path continued beyond the large stone. Finally, the girls saw the end of the tunnel. Janie stopped short. Claire, not paying attention, bumped into her.

"Sorry," Claire said as she took a step back.

"Shh," Janie said softly.

"What?" Claire whispered.

"Listen," Janie said and the girls both listened to what sounded like huffing and puffing.

"I have heard that sound before. I know what it is. I know why I have the sword," she said with wide eyes. "That is a Cinderbeast."

"And it doesn't sound happy," Janie made a face, "or pleasant."

"It is not. When the Ogres used to attack Fluberbia, many of them rode in on Cinderbeasts. Cinderbeasts are the most ferocious of creatures. They are as large as a mountain is wide, with fanged teeth and poisonous taluses on their long tails and they throw fire from their fingers and noses when angered and they are always angry."

"Swell," Janie gulped as she moved ahead towards the outside.

Claire held up the sword. "I should go first."

"Let's go together," Janie suggested and the girls stepped back out into the sunlight shaded by the forest of flowers and directly in front of the largest, most frightening creature, Janie had ever seen.

Claire took a step forward towards the great beast.

It roared loudly and reared its head towards the heavens. Fire spewed from its giant nostrils and singed the delicate flower petals canopying the small clearing.

Janie trembled and sweat streamed down Claire's face, but she did not flinch. She held up the sword and the beast turned and waved its massive tail, swatting at the girls.

Claire jumped as high as she could, as Janie ducked back into the rosebush cave, and the tail swished by them.

The next wave of the Cinderbeast's tail was higher. This time Claire ducked, but held up the sword. Blood trickled from the beast's tail.

"You nicked him," Janie called. "Hold it in front of you."

Claire put the sword in front of her and lunged forward expertly.

"Whoa!" Janie said.

Claire advanced and lunged again. The Cinderbeast reared angrily and flared back, taking a deep breath, ready to spray fire over the girls.

Claire saw the exposed chest and took a swipe, pulled back and thrust her sword into the midsection of the animal as he was coming down upon her.

The beast howled so loudly the forest quaked. He stumbled. Claire grabbed the sword again with both hands, struggled to pull it out of the scaly underside and once again pierced the beast's thick, gray skin.

The ferocious fiend fell in a pounding thump. Smoke seeped and sizzled from its nose, mouth and fingers but it was not breathing.

Janie slowly joined Claire, who hovered over the beast in shock and awe.

"Nice work!" Janie patted Claire's back without taking her eyes off the giant form in front of them.

"Holy cow!" Claire said, wiping her brow with the back of her hand. "That was not fun."

"Amazing," Janie said.

The girls just stood and stared a long, long time.

"Think we should look at the riddle again?" Janie asked.

"Oh yes," Claire said, coming out of her trance but only slightly.

"You slayed a Cinderbeast," Janie put her arm around her friend and led her past the beast.

"It looks as if I did," Claire said matter-of-factly.

"My brother would think this is so cool!" Janie said. Her heart sank a little. She missed her family.

Janie pulled out the map. "Do you think it is a little odd how the first riddle was on parchment and the rest on this ultra-modern 3-D map?"

"Not really," Claire shrugged, "Fluberbia is a mixture of old and new. It is a delicate balance."

Janie returned to the riddle. *"Golden yellow, blue and pink. Something to eat, upon which to think. Open the door, built by no man, grill up the fire – rocks in the pan."*

"Don't think this is creepy, but look back at the Cinderbeast. He is turning pink," Claire said.

Janie looked over her shoulder. The Cinderbeast was indeed turning pink and shrinking. Smaller, smaller, smaller the beast became. When it was the size of a monarch butterfly, it sprouted wings, popped up and floated through the air.

"This is the weirdest place I have ever been in my whole entire life," Janie said. "No offense," she said to Claire – not wanting to hurt her new friend's feelings.

They turned back up the path and stopped. For there in front of them, carved into a large daffodil, was what appeared to be a door.

"Really!" Janie said in a surprised sarcastic tone, because nothing about this place actually did surprise her at all.

"Carved by no man," Claire added. "It looks like it is part of the flower. Open it up."

Janie carefully took hold of the green handle and turned. The door popped open and rocks tumbled out.

Janie and Claire quickly gathered them up.

"Look around," Claire said, "do you see a pan or a fire?"

"We can build a fire, we need the pan," Janie said. Something out of the corner of her eye caught her attention. It was the butterfly, or cinderfly to be exact.

It flitted and fluttered – as if beckoning them to follow.

"I think it wants us to follow him," Claire said.

Name: _____ Date: _____ #: _____

The Cinderbeast Story Map

Title:
Who - Who is in the chapter "The Cinderbeast"?   ---
Where - Where does this chapter take place?   ---
Beginning - What happens in the beginning?   ---   ---
Middle - What happens in the middle of the chapter?   ---   ---
End - how does this chapter end?   ---   ---

The Cinderbeast Cause and Effect

This chapter is a great one to show cause and effect.

Cause - when something happens   Effect - What happens

Choose two things that happen in *The Cinderbeast* and then list the effects of what happened.

Cause:

Effect:

Cause:

Effect:

The Cinderbeast Questions for Comprehension

1. Who was proud to carry the special sword?
   a. Claire
   b. Julia
   c. The Cinderbeast
   d. Julia

2. Who was making the huffing and puffing sound?
   a. the ogre
   b. the Cinderbeast
   c. Princess Claire
   d. the frog

3. The beast howled so loudly, what happened to the forest?
   a. it quaked
   b. it rumbled
   c. it burned
   d. it rolled.

4. The door was carved into what?
   a. a tree
   b. the Cinderbeast's tail
   c. a violet
   d. a daffodil

5. What does the riddle tell Princess Claire and Janie to put into a pan?
   a. roses
   b. fire
   c. wood
   d. rocks

6. Summarize the chapter titled *"The Cinderbeast"* in five sentences:

_____

_____

_____

_____

_____

_____

_____

Chapter 15: Another One Down

They cautiously let the cinderfly lead them off the path.

"Wait!" Claire called, "the sword." The sword lay on the ground. Claire picked it up and carried it with them. "Just in case," she said when she caught up with Janie. "You just never know."

"You can say that again," Janie agreed.

The cinderfly led them to a colorful patch of tall tulips – large enough to be trees. The ground was blanketed with azaleas – vibrantly pink and red.

In the center of the patch were rocks arranged in a circle.

The cinderfly, that was once the great Cinderbeast, floated across the circle and the logs, set inside, blazed to life.

The cinderfly landed upon the fire and flashed and sputtered and flipped – turning itself into a frying pan.

"The rocks," Claire said as she knelt down by the fire.

Janie handed Claire the rocks. It seemed fitting the princess who slayed the beast, or at least who just turned it into a cinderfly, do the honors.

Claire carefully placed the rocks in the pan. They started to smoke and to sizzle and to melt and to blend, they turned green, then black, then gray and finally blue – sapphire blue.

The fire flashed and the cinderfly turned into the head of Ephora and this time she was smiling as the beauteous blue gem found its way into the filling crown.

Active Reading

Text detail: Why does the author use the word cautiously here?

Hint: What has happened to make caution necessary?

_____
_____
_____
_____
_____
_____
_____
_____
_____
_____

Circle the most important five words on this page and explain why you think they are important.

_____
_____
_____
_____
_____
_____
_____

As quickly as it appeared, it was gone. The soft bed under them was now dirt. The fabulous field of flowers was no more.

The girls looked around and, sure enough all of the flowers had vanished. Their succulent scent lingered, as if they might need proof it ever existed.

Before them was a sea of snot – a hot, bubbling, thick, grossly green sea of snot. It was thick and slimy and smelled like mint. Mint snot!

Protruding high above the snot, high above the ground on the other side of the tumbling, molten mixture, were the mountains of Ne'r'goup – tall and pristine, and above the highest peak, was the tower.

Claire's breath caught in her chest and her heart stopped. "Mother and father," she whispered with a tear in her eye.

Janie put her arm around the princess' shoulder. "We're almost there," she said softly.

The snot spurted and gurgled. "After we get through that!" Claire said.

"There's always something," Janie huffed, shaking her head. "Any suggestions?"

"The map," Claire said, "do we have a new riddle?"

Think and Write

How does this chapter move the plot of the story forward? Remember the plot is what happens in a story.

_____

_____

_____

_____

_____

_____

_____

_____

_____

_____

Chapter 16: Almost There

The map sprang to life when Janie rolled it open and laid it out before them. The points at which they found the other gems were pulsating in an orchestra of light and sound.

The next and final riddle popped up where they were – at the mouth of the great Snot Pit of Ne'r'goup.

"*Back you turn, left then right. A journey of day not into the night. A race against time, a refuge gone bad. A monkey, a rhino and a brown bear so sad,*" Janie read. "That doesn't make sense. Is it saying we have to turn back. Are there animals in the Enchanted Forest we have to find?"

"Nothing lives in the Enchanted Forest but Cinderbeasts," Claire said.

"Oh no! Does that mean we have to go back through the forest?"

The girls stared at the map. They were at the mouth of the great Snot Pit of Ne'r'goup and that was at the top left corner of the map.

"Turn it over," Claire instructed.

"But the back is blank," Janie said, looking at the other side of the virtual map.

"Not really, spread it out and I'll show you," Claire said.

Janie flipped the map and smoothed it out – making sure to stretch its corners. Instantly, it came alive. This time the *you are here* spot was in the bottom left corner and a new section of the map was revealed.

"This is a very cool map," Janie said.

Claire smiled proudly. "My dad helped invent the technology. Our maps used to be boring. They just sat there – flat and still. My dad had this idea for books and maps and directories to be completely interactive and this is what happened."

"He must be pretty smart," Janie said.

"Apparently not smart enough to keep his aunt happy," Claire rolled her eyes. "I miss them," she said softly.

"I miss my family too, but we are almost done." She looked at the map. "Let's see, *monkey, rhinos and a sad brown bear.*"

Claire pointed to a spot in the center of the map. "The Old Animal Refuge!"

"The what?" Janie asked.

"The Old Animal Refuge. We read about it in school. It's where all of the animals from the Kingdom of Ephora go when they are too old to be useful."

"Too old to be useful," Janie was confused. How could anything be thought of as being too old to be useful?

"My great aunt has several quirks. One of them is all of the animals in her kingdom, even the wild ones, must be young and spry. She keeps them all in a zoo and when they get too old for her she sends them to The Old Animal Refuge. That is where we have to go."

Janie stretched out on the ground and looked up at the Fluberbian sky. She loved the giant puffy clouds and the blueness of the air.

She learned in school, the blue is from molecules. They swim around in the air and scatter blue light from the sun. They did an experiment, in her class, where they filled a glass with water and a tiny bit of milk. When they shined a flashlight through the milk, the droplets turned blue – just like the molecules in the air.

"You can feel the heat from the snot," Janie said, "and that mint smell is overwhelming."

"I can see the tower," Claire pointed to the top of Ne'r'goup.

"Do you think there's another way to get to your parents?" Janie turned towards the princess and leaned up on one elbow.

"You mean besides going all the way to the refuge and back?" Claire asked.

"Yes, I mean, we are already this close. Maybe we can find a way across the snot and help them break out," she said doubtfully, but she was tired.

"I think we need to follow the rules," Claire said.

Claire was a brilliant child, full of common sense. She knew there would never be true peace and that none of them would ever be free until someone put the crown back together. She knew it was the fight between her great aunt and her immediate family that was the real issue.

"So we're going to the refuge," Janie said weakly.

Claire stood and this time she helped Janie up. "It's this way," she headed east around the snot.

"Are you taking that?" Janie asked of the sword Claire was carrying.

"We might need it. Really it isn't heavy for me," the princess said.

Janie went to the edge of the pit and tugged at a lovely and fragrant flowery vine. She quickly looped it around itself and tied a knot. "Let's make a holder, so you can carry it over your shoulder."

She put her creation over Claire's shoulder and the sword fit in perfectly at her waist.

"Wow, this is cool. How did you know how to do this?" Claire asked knowing swords were not a big part of life on earth.

"I'm pretty crafty. I can make anything," Janie shrugged. "Are we off?"

"We are off," Claire said and the girls followed the dirt road to The Old Animal Refuge.

Both the snot and the Enchanted Forest formed a circle around the Mountains of Ne'r'goup and the path they traveled to the refuge took them on a narrow route between the two.

Claire kept her eye on the forest as she walked. Waiting for the flowers to reappear – only they didn't.

Janie had been watching Claire walk for their entire journey and, if the truth be known, the girl didn't pay very close attention to her steps and sort of tripped over a lot of things. It made Janie nervous to watch the princess walk on the edge of the snot.

"Claire, I know you are a princess and all and have been running a kingdom all by yourself, but you are making me very nervous," she said.

"Why?" Claire asked at the same moment she stumbled, once again, on nothing except the ground itself.

"That's why," Janie pointed out. "Could you please walk on the forest side? You are way too close to the snot and..."

Claire interrupted with a laugh, but moved to the other side of Janie – just as Janie tripped over a small rock herself.

"No offense," Claire chuckled, "but you are not so sure footed either, my friend. Perhaps we should both avoid the edge."

The girls needed the laughter. It made them feel better, so much so they talked and laughed all the way to the gates of The Old Animal Refuge.

They had a lot in common and finally felt like this journey was going to be victorious for them. They were so close.

They stopped laughing immediately when they reached the gates of the depressing refuge.

The gate was tall and old and rusty and the fence, surrounding the area within, was made from an odd mix of bamboo and razor wire – sharp and foreboding.

Inside, the ground was in contrast to the Enchanted Forest now surrounding it on three sides.

"The forest flowers are back," Janie noted.

Animals wandered, searching for grass upon which to graze and water to drink, but none seemed to be around.

"They all look sad," Claire said.

Almost There Questions for Comprehension

1. According to Princess Claire, what is the only thing that lives in the Enchanted Forest?
      a. Cinderflies
      b. Cinderbeasts
      c. butterflies
      d. princesses

2. According to Princess Claire, who helped invent the map technology?
      a. Princess Julia
      b. Miloph
      c. the king
      d. Princess Claire.

3. Where does the riddle in this chapter send the girls?
      a. the quarry
      b. the zoo
      c. the old animal refuge
      d. Fluberbia

4. What do Janie and Princess Claire use to make a holder for the sword?
      a. a jacket
      b. a bag
      c. a vine
      d. a backpack

5. Why does Janie ask Princess Claire to walk on the forest side of the path?

_____

_____

6. Summarize the chapter titled *"The Cinderbeast"* in five sentences:

_____

_____

_____

_____

_____

_____

Name: _____ Date: _____ #: _____

Almost There Character Trading Cards

Choose two characters from Fluberbia and create trading cards. Draw a picture on the front and use character traits on the back as part of your description.

You may also use this link to make digital trading cards: http://www.readwritethink.org/classroom-resources/mobile-apps/trading-cards-30922.html

Chapter 17: The Old Animal Refuge

"Is this where your animals go?" Janie asked, her heart breaking for the lonely and ill-fed creatures on the other side of the fence.

"No, our animals just live. No zoos, no boundaries. They live like we do – free to roam as long as they don't hurt anyone, but that is a two way street. We are good to them and they are good to us." Claire said. "These poor things."

A wrinkled, gray elephant labored towards them. "Hallo," he said.

Janie was surprised he could speak. Claire was not. All of the animals in Fluberbia and the world beyond – this world at least – could speak. They were not all nice, nor where they all very smart, but they all could speak.

"Hello, friend," Claire said.

"Friend you say? Huh!" he said. "Look what your people did to us. Look around you. You are no friend to us." He turned to leave.

"Wait!" Claire called. "I am Princess Claire of Fluberbia."

The elephant stopped and turned. "You are not of the Kingdom of Ephora? For they are the only souls who visit – with more animals too old to be of use to them."

"No, we are here from Fluberbia," Claire said again.

"You treat our kind well there," he said wistfully. "We all dream of your land."

"We are here to help you," Janie said.

Claire stepped back and gave the other girl a surprised look.

Janie turned to her. "We have to. We have to find the diamond, rescue your parents and then rescue them."

"I don't know. Ephora might get angry," Claire said.

"And do what? Curse you? Kidnap your parents?" Janie said sarcastically.

"You make a very good point."

"We can't just leave them here."

The elephant's ears perked up and other animals began to gather around him. A lion, a tiger, monkeys, bears, all sad, all docile.

"We are not ferocious here," the lion said.

"Will you really help us?" an old gorilla asked as she climbed on the gate.

"Of course we will," said the princess. "Only we have to rescue my parents first."

"We have to find the diamond and to do that we need to solve a riddle about a sad bear."

A bear approached. "We are all sad here." She moved her friends aside, the gorilla got off the gate and the bear opened it up for the girls.

"Wait, you're not locked in?" Janie asked. "Why don't you just leave?"

"And go where?" the gorilla asked.

"We tired that long ago, but there is nothing for us outside. Our plan was to make our way to Fluberbia, but the Cinderbeasts are massive and skilled fighters and no one could make it through alive."

"We'll get you through," said the girls in unison.

"And I will take you to the diamond," the bear said.

The elephant pounded his large front leg – once, twice. All looked at him. He raised his trunk and spoke loudly. "We cannot part with the diamond. It is our only hope for salvation," he looked at the girls. "I trust you will try to help us, but the once back King of Fluberbia asked us to guard the gem and said not to part with it as it will one day be our salvation."

Claire's eyes got wide. "I think he meant us."

Janie looked at her.

Claire spoke again. "I think it is all part of the plan." She turned back to the animals. "The once back king was my grandfather and I think, in some way, he has sent me. On my word as the Princess of Fluberbia – you will all be saved. Where is the lion?"

A mangy old lion, with still a twinkle in his tired eyes, approached.

"Are you not the king of the animal kingdom?" Claire asked.

"Indeed, that should be the case," he said regally.

Claire took off her vine casing with the sword inside. "This is a magical sword and near as we can determine, the only thing to defeat the wild Cinderbeasts. We know it works. We defeated one to get here. If you trade us the diamond – I will leave the sword for you to hold until we come back."

"Claire!" Janie realized what the other girl was saying, "we can't get back through the Enchanted Forest without it!"

"Then we have to come back don't we?" she said confidently and the animals believed her heart was pure.

The gorilla approached. "Can you walk on the violets?" he asked.

"We both can," Claire said softly.

The gorilla held out his hand in a gesture of friendship and Claire took it. "Bear," said the gorilla, "please take them to the diamond."

The diamond rested in an ornately carved wooden case – hidden in the trunk of an old tree. It glistened in the sweltering, dry sun.

Claire reached for it. When she touched the glistening gem, it did not dance and the crown did not appear. Her heart sank. She turned to Janie.

"It must not be the one. The vision didn't appear, the crown did not complete."

Janie thought. "Wait! It said we needed it to part the snot. Maybe it will return to the crown after that."

The gorilla picked it up and handed it to Claire. "Try and we will wait here for you to return."

Claire took the diamond and thanked her new friends. The animals walked the girls to the gate.

"Don't forget us," said the elephant.

Claire walked to him and hugged his trunk. "Not in a million years.

The girls exited gate – waving to their new friends.

"We'll see you soon," Claire called.

Janie held her hand out to the lion. "Guide them well your majesty."

The lion smiled. He had not been called that in a long time.

Name: _____ Date: _____ #: _____

Comprehension Questions for Critical Thinking: *"The Old Animal Refuge"*

Answer the following questions using complete sentences.

1. Describe the first animal that approached Princess Claire and Janie.

2. What is the last gem the girls must find?

3. Name at least four different types of animals held in the refuge.

4. What kept the animals from Fluberbia?

5. What do the girls leave with the animals and why?

6. What is different about when they find the last gem?

Name: _____ Date: _____ #: _____

Dictionary Skills - Fluberbia So Far

Look up the following words and write the definitions below.

Word	Definition
struggle	
frantic	
frightened	
tussle	
ferocious	

Scan back through the story and write down any words, so far, that you are unsure of. Look up their definitions and write them below

Word	Definition

Main Idea: The Old Animal Refuge

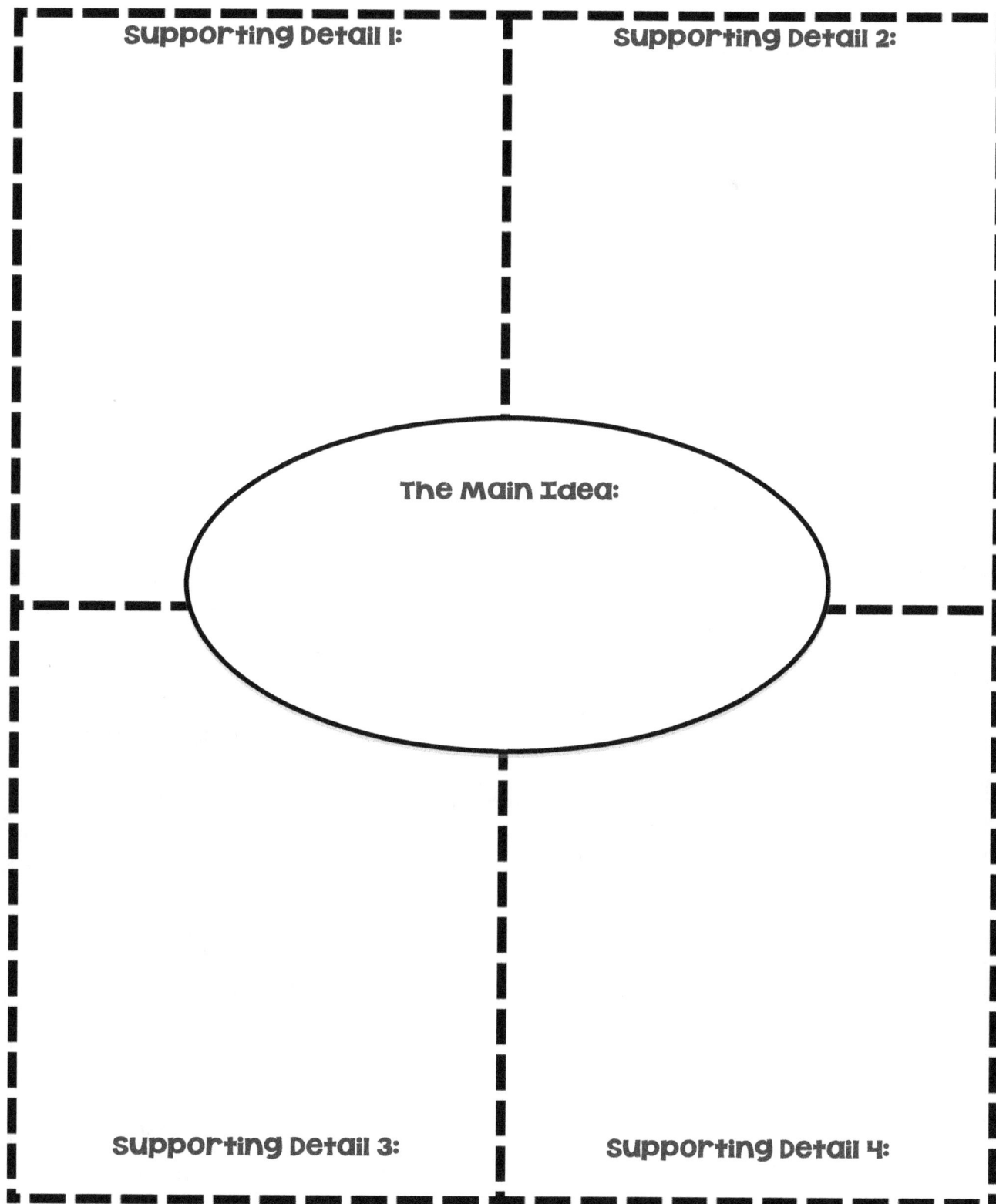

Supporting Detail 1:

Supporting Detail 2:

The Main Idea:

Supporting Detail 3:

Supporting Detail 4:

Performance Task 4: *Stimulus Text:*

Read this text and then answer the prompt that follows it.

The Old Animal Refuge
From <u>Fluberbia</u>

Claire took off her vine casing with the sword inside. "This is a magical sword and near as we can determine, the only thing to defeat the wild Cinderbeasts. We know it works. We defeated one to get here. If you trade us the diamond – I will leave the sword for you to hold until we come back."

"Claire!" Janie realized what the other girl was saying, "we can't get back through the Enchanted Forest without it!"

"Then we have to come back don't we?" she said confidently and the animals believed her heart was pure.

The gorilla approached. "Can you walk on the violets?" he asked.

"We both can," Claire said softly.

The gorilla held out his hand in a gesture of friendship and Claire took it. "Bear," said the gorilla, "please take them to the diamond."

The diamond rested in an ornately carved wooden case – hidden in the trunk of an old tree. It glistened in the sweltering, dry sun.

Claire reached for it. When she touched the glistening gem, it did not dance and the crown did not appear. Her heart sank. She turned to Janie.

"It must not be the one. The vision didn't appear, the crown did not complete."

Janie thought. "Wait! It said we needed it to part the snot. Maybe it will return to the crown after that."

The gorilla picked it up and handed it to Claire. "Try and we will wait here for you to return."

Claire took the diamond and thanked her new friends. The animals walked the girls to the gate.

"Don't forget us," said the elephant.

Claire walked to him and hugged his trunk. "Not in a million years.

The girls exited gate – waving to their new friends.

"We'll see you soon," Claire called.

Janie held her hand out to the lion. "Guide them well your majesty."

The lion smiled. He had not been called that in a long time.

Item Prompt:

The author shows that the animals trust Princess Claire and Janie. Write a paragraph telling how you know the animals trust the girls. Use specific details from the story to support your answer.

Item Prompt 2:

Draw content of the stimulus text in four panels.

Use this template to organize your thoughts before you write your paragraph.

Performance Task Graphic Organizer	
Fluberbia: The Old Animal Refuge	
Main idea of your paragraph	
Evidence 1 showing the animals trust the girls	
Support for Evidence 1	
Evidence 2 showing the animals trust the girls	
Support for Evidence 2	
Evidence 3 showing Janie is curious	
Support for Evidence 3	
Conclusion	

Performance Task Rubric

	Scoring Rubric
3	The response: • Gives sufficient evidence of student's ability to use supporting evidence to interpret and explain inferences about a character • Includes specific explanations that make reference to the text • Fully supports the interfaces with clearly relevant details from the text
2	The response: • Gives some evidence of the ability to use supporting evidence to interpret and explain inferences about a character. • Includes some specific explanations that make reference to the text. • Adequately supports the inferences with clearly relevant details from the text.
1	The response: • Gives limited evidence of the ability to use supporting evidence to interpret and explain inferences about a character • Includes specific explanations but they are not explicit or make only vague references to the text. • Supports the inferences with at least one detail but the relevance of that detail to the text must be inferred
0	The response: A response gets no credit if it provides no evidence of the ability to use supporting evidence to interpret and explain inferences about a character and includes no relevant information from the text.

The Snot and the Diamond

Janie and Claire stopped at the edge of the great Snot Pit of Ne'r'goup and looked up at the tower. The heat from the bubbling, churning, molten liquid caused sweat to bead on their brows.

Claire pulled the diamond from her pocket and out fell the kerchief her sister gave her for the journey. It wiggled and moved. It seemed alive.

"Ah, Claire," Janie lifted her eyebrow at the moving cloth, "are handkerchief's alive here too?"

Claire looked down. "Not that I know of."

Both girls jumped back when twin Julia, the fairy princess, popped out of the folded cloth.

"Whoa!" Julia exclaimed, just as surprised as the others she was there.

"How'd you get here?" Claire asked hugging her sister.

"We're at the pit," Julia noticed excitely. "You did it!"

"Almost," Claire said, hugging her sister again, "but how did you get here?"

"I wished it so when I tucked the handkerchief secretly in your pocket. Then, today I said the old incantation that never worked before," Julia answered, "apparently it works now."

"Don't you see?" Janie said, her eyes dancing with excitement. "Your magic is starting to work!"

"Oh Janie," Julia said, "that means you will be able to go home soon!"

Claire tilted her head to one side and looked at Janie. "But I don't want you to go," the princess said. "I will miss you greatly."

Janie put her hands on the princess' shoulders. "I'll miss you too, but I miss my family so much. I have to go home."

Their conversation was interrupted by a whizzing noise of sorts. The diamond rumbled and moved. The great Snot Pit surrounding the Mountains of Ne'r'goup parted and pieces of the tower fell upon them as it crumbled and rumbled down the high mountain.

"Cover your heads!" Janie cried – diving to protect the princesses.

For a final time, the vision of Ephora appeared. The crown shined in its complete brilliance and the image spoke.

"You have done well my grand niece. You, and the chosen one from the land beyond the flower, have brought peace back to our kingdom," her great aunt smiled and the image began to fade. "You will know her true name and the ties to our land when the time is right."

"Wait!" Janie called and then turned to Claire, "the animals."

"Oh yes," Claire approached the waning vision. "Does peace and harmony mean the animals too? May we have their freedom and the promise that all of the animals from the Kingdom of Ephora will have the same life as those from the Kingdom of Fluberbia?"

"I can agree to that," Ephora said, "on one condition."

"What is that?" asked Claire.

"That can wait," Ephora said as the image faded.

"Girls!" came a cry from halfway up the mountain.

They looked up and their parents were running to them.

"Mother! Father!" they cried in unison and raced towards the now free King and Queen of Fluberbia.

Only Julia stumbled. Janie approached to help her up. Her smile was wide.

"The wings are gone," Janie said.

Julia breathed a sigh of relief, hugged Janie and raced to her parents.

Janie watched happily as the reunited, royal family transcended the mountain towards her.

When at the bottom, the king looked at Janie.

"So, you are the one," he said nobly.

"That's what they tell me," Janie smiled a bit shyly.

"Our debt of gratitude can never be repaid," he said.

Janie winked at Claire. "It was nothing."

They both giggled feverishly.

"Come," he said, "our kingdom awaits."

"But Father," Claire said, "there is one more thing."

"And what is that?" he asked.

"Janie must get home," she said.

Janie felt all nervous inside. What if she coldn't? What if there really was no way home?

"That is easy," the queen said. "Just close your eyes, turn three times and wish it so."

"That's it?" Janie asked. "I knew it!" she exclaimed.

"Knew what?" Claire asked.

"Like Dorothy. It was there all the time," she said.

"Dorothy again? You're pretty obsessed with her."

Janie laughed. "Naw, more like obsessed with getting home."

"We hope," the King said, "you will stay for the celebration and the knighting. After all, it is you we will be honoring."

The twins jumped up and down and danced around Janie.

"It is my intention," he continued, "to make you a Royal Knight of the Fluberbian Court. It is also my intention to reveal to you the one true way you can revisit us again and again and again."

"I'd like that," Janie said.

"Let's go get the animals and go home," Claire said.

"Animals?" the queen asked.

"It's a long story," Claire said. "I'll tell you on the way."

Arm in arm they walked towards the refuge.

"What day is it?" the king suddenly asked as they approached the gates of The Old Animal Refuge.

"December 31, I think," Julia said.

"If we hurry home, my dears, we will only miss the first quarter of the big Fluberbian championship! After which will be the perfect time for a celebration."

Claire hugged her father as they walked. "And you will never have to miss another first quarter so long as you live."

"Janie," Julia called the girl from the land beyond the flower aside. "What do you suppose Ephora meant about the animals and the condition?"

"I am sure we'll find out," Janie said – looking forward to the celebration and most of all, the knowledge that she would be spending this night, snuggled safely and securely in her own bed.

The Snot and the Diamond Questions for Comprehension

1. The kerchief wiggled and moved and came alive. What was in it?
   a. a Cinderfly
   b. a rock
   c. an Ogre fairy
   d. Princess Julia

2. After the Ephora appears and the last gem finishes the crown, Ephora says:
   a. "You have done well my grand niece."
   b. "We will never have peace."
   c. "We are family again."
   d. "Here is the key to the tower."

3. What does Claire ask her aunt?
   a. for Cinderbeast freedom
   b. to come and live in the Kingdom of Fluberbia
   c. to free the animals
   d. to give up the crown

4. On what date do the girls arrive at the tower?
   a. December 31
   b. January 1
   c. December 23
   d. December 11

5. Describe your favorite part of this chapter?

_____

_____

_____

6. Summarize the chapter titled *"The Snot and the Diamond"* in five sentences:

_____

_____

_____

_____

_____

_____

_____

End of Book Assessment

Comprehension Cut-Outs

Comprehension Cut-Outs are a great way to test student comprehension of the story. They can even be used as an assessment – in chapter clusters or all together.

Have students cut out the "Comprehension Cut-Outs" and re-assemble them in the order they appear in the chapter. Once cut-outs are in order, have students attach them to a page in their notebooks.

Instruct students to cut out the "comprehension cut-outs" and put them together based on how the story progresses or team students up, mix all of the chapters together and have students try to reassemble them as a team. Playing the Jeopardy theme music while they try to un-scramble them is a fun way to assess group work!

Differentiation: There are three blank panels, have more advanced students add events from the story to the cut-outs and arrange their events along with the others.

Comprehension Cut-Outs – End of Book Test
Clip the Comprehension Cut-Outs and arrange the sentences in the order they progress through the story.

1 Claire easily pulled the sword from out of the giant rock.	2. Janie fell through a flower and ended up in the Kingdom of Fluberbia	3. The diamond parted the snot!	4. Everything was different in Fluberbia...even the food moved.
5. They promised the animals they would be back to help free them.	6. Popperas left the girls at the edge of the Enchanted Forest.	7. The Cinderbeast was large and frightening	8. They had to back-track to the animal refuge.
9. Flash frantically swam towards Janie and nudged her to shore.	10. They were surprised to see Goloph with the Ogres.	11. Miloph was the keeper of the parchment, on it was the first riddle.	12. The Cinderbeast turned into a Cinderfly.
13. The Cinderfly turned into a sapphire.	14. The bird, Popperas, swept down and called to Janie.	15. The reached the Gulch of Doom when the sun was still high in the sky.	16. They rescued the King and Queen.

Appendix A
Rubrics for scoring
And...answers

Rubric for Socratic Seminar – Whole Class

Use this rubric to track what student say during a Socratic Seminar. In the far left column, write the names of students who are in the circle and place point in the middle column. Use the far right column as a tally.

Students in the Circle	Asks higher level question	Refers back to text	Refers to another student's ideas	Offers a useful comment	Total score
Students in the Hot Seat – Those who enter to participate					

Name: _____ **Date:** _____

Please attach assignment

Rubric for Constructed Response Questions

Score	Description	Score Tally
4	Response answered the question, relates to the reading and student has a grasp of the main story element (s) applicable.	
3	Response answers the question, relates to the reading and student has a grasp of the main story element(s) applicable – but complete sentences were not used and there are problems with spelling and/or grammar.	
2	Response provides a partial answer with limited, incomplete or partially correct information	
1	Response is minimal or vague.	
0	No or incorrect response.	

Teacher Comments: _____

_____

_____

_____

_____

Student Comments: _____

_____

_____

_____

_____

Answers

The following are sample answers. Please use *Rubric* for all constructed response questions as answer will vary. Student answers should be in complete sentences, free of errors. Explaining this is part of the grade and providing feedback reinforces the CCSS.

Page 25: 1. Crystal clear days, when the sky is blue and the clouds are puffy, soft and bouncy. 2. Play around town and explore. They play in the parks and the fairgrounds – pirates and other games. 3. A special plant that blooms into a violet. Janie falls through the violet. 4. Predictions will vary.

Page 30: 1. Princess Julia is magical and has fairy characteristics. 2. They were kidnapped and put in a tower by Princess Julia's evil aunt. 3. Answers should include how Janie reacts to her surroundings and how Julia reacts to Janie. Answers will vary. 4. Predictions will vary.

Page 41: 1. The violet path come and goes. The flowers only bloom for special people to walk on. 2.triangular and symmetrical and pink and purple – with gold gilding. 3. Kidnapped them and locked them in a tower. 4. Answers will vary. 5. Give the people the things they need. 6. Heated pools, electricity, television, the internet, etc.

Page 42: 1. "What's with the path?" she asked Julia. 2. Princess Julia walked easily along the path. 3. Janie and Julia both went to the beautiful palace. 4. The girls walked together as the flowers opened up before them. 5. The palace was big, pink and gold. Janie thought it was pretty. (or ... big, pink, and gold).

Page 51: 1. Apples of pure, polished rubies. 2. The kitchen was a contradiction. A kettle brewed over an open fire, but there was a wall of televisions. Nothing made sense. 3. Fluberbian butter is alive. It moves. 4. "...go through the forest, over the snot, up the mountain and rescue the parents..." 5. Up the stairs to find something for Janie to wear. 6. Miloph.

Page 60: 1. Miloph is a bird. 2. Parchment is paper. 3. Find something that will lead them to the next riddle. 4. Princess Julia and Princess Claire are running Fluberbia. 5. The prince of the Ogres has the emerald they will need. 6. By finding all of the gems for the Crown of Goodness that were scattered.

Page 61: 4,1,2,5,3

Page 68: 1. Nothing. Janie was able to touch the parchment. 2. Another riddle. 3. An empty crown appeared on Ephora's suspended head – the ruby returned to its place. 4. The map is alive.

Page 86: 1. Claire. 2. They are mean, magical and work in mines. They are evil and tricky, but they are slow.

Page 93: 1. A horse. 2. Pulling Claire out of the water. 3. It received an odd text – even though texts were usually blocked. 4. "The only think green down there are the trees covering the doors in the ground." 5. Because Claire's parents were kidnapped and she and her sister were running the kingdom. 6. Adults would figure things out if they treated others like they wanted to be treated.

Page 99: 1. Goloph. 2. Answers will vary – remember they stayed in Goloph's house. 3. Rode Flash. 4. They dive-bombed the Ogres and then they rode one away.

Page 105: 1. Because the main setting is an enchanted forest. 2. Ne'r'goup. 3. The tower in which Claire's parents are held prisoner is there. 4. Janie can't budge it, but Claire easily removes it from a rock. 5. Remove the sword and carry it.

Page 106: 3,5,1,2,4

Page 107: 1. Princess Claire and Janie walked through the forest. 2. Janie wondered if she would ever get home again. 3. Princess Claire found the sword in a large rock. 4. The enchanted forest was full of trees.

Page 113: 1. A 2. B. 3. A. 4. D 5. D.

Page 120: 1. A. 2. C. 3. C. 4. C. 5. She doesn't want her to trip and fall.

Page 125: 1. A wrinkled, gray elephant. 2. The diamond. 3. Monkeys, elephants, lions, bears… 4. The animals in Fluberbia just live. 5. Claire leaves the sword. They all know the sword is needed to get back through the Enchanted forest, so she leaves it so the animals know she will come back for them. 6. It does not instantly make the crown appear.

Page 135: 1. D. 2. A. 3. C. 4. A.

Page 137: 2,4,11,9,15,10,14,6,1,7,12,13,8,5,3,16

Appendix B
Math Task Cards
for Centers or Anytime

Fluberbia
Task Card 1
3.OA.D.8

Janie now knew the violets that grew near Zia's were magical. She also knew they were growing quickly. Janie saw 3 new violets per day for the days she stayed at Zia's. She ended with 12 violets in all.

How many violets were there after 3 four days?

a. Write an equation to match the problem. Use the letter v to stand for the missing number.

b. Solve the problem. Explain how you found the answer.

Fluberbia
Task Card 1
3.OA.D.8 -- Solution

Janie now knew the violets that grew near Zia's were magical. She also knew they were growing quickly. Janie saw 3 new violets per day for the days she stayed at Zia's. She ended with 12 violets in all.

How many violets were there after 3 four days?

a. Write an equation to match the problem. Use the letter v to stand for the missing number. $3 \times v = 12$

b. Solve the problem. Explain how you found the answer.
v = 4. If Janie has 3 new violets per day and ends with 12, I know I have to divide

Fluberbia
Task Card 2
3.NBT.A.2

The Giants traveled 622 yards from the Great Palace of Fluberbia to meet Janie. Then they walked 423 yards back before they stopped at the drawbridge. How many yards did they walk in all?

hundreds	tens	ones
6	2	2
+ 4	2	3

Fluberbia
Task Card 2
3.NBT.A.2 - Solution

The Giants traveled 622 yards from the Great Palace of Fluberbia to meet Janie. Then they walked 423 yards back before they stopped at the drawbridge. How many yards did they walk in all?

hundreds	tens	ones
6	2	2
+ 4	2	3
10	4	5

Task Card 3
3.NBT.A.2

The creature walked 360 degrees around Janie. Then the creature walked 167 degrees back the other way. How many degrees did the creature walk in all?

hundreds	tens	ones
3	6	0
+ 1	6	7

Fluberbia
Task Card 3
3.NBT.A.2 - Solution

The creature walked 360 degrees around Janie. Then the creature walked 167 degrees back the other way. How many degrees did the creature walk in all?

hundreds	tens	ones
^{1}3	6	0
+ 1	6	7
5	2	7

Fluberbia
Task Card 4
3.NBT.A.2

Ephoria is a kingdom near Fluberbia. Ephoria is 316 miles from Fluberbia over land and 142 miles over water.

If Janie and Princess Julia traveled to Ephoria from Fluberia over land and returned by boat, how far would have travelled in all?

hundreds	tens	ones
3	1	6
+ 1	4	2

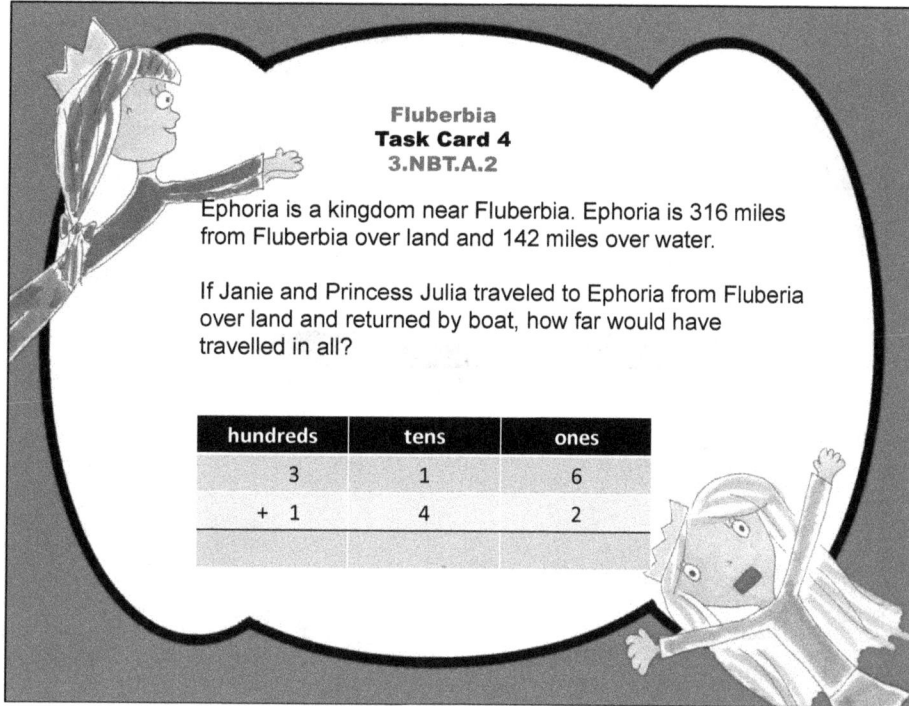

Fluberbia
Task Card 4
3.NBT.A.2 - Solution

Ephoria is a kingdom near Fluberbia. Ephoria is 316 miles from Fluberbia over land and 142 miles over water.

If Janie and Princess Julia traveled to Ephoria from Fluberia over land and returned by boat, how far would have travelled in all?

hundreds	tens	ones
3	1	6
+ 1	4	2
4	5	8

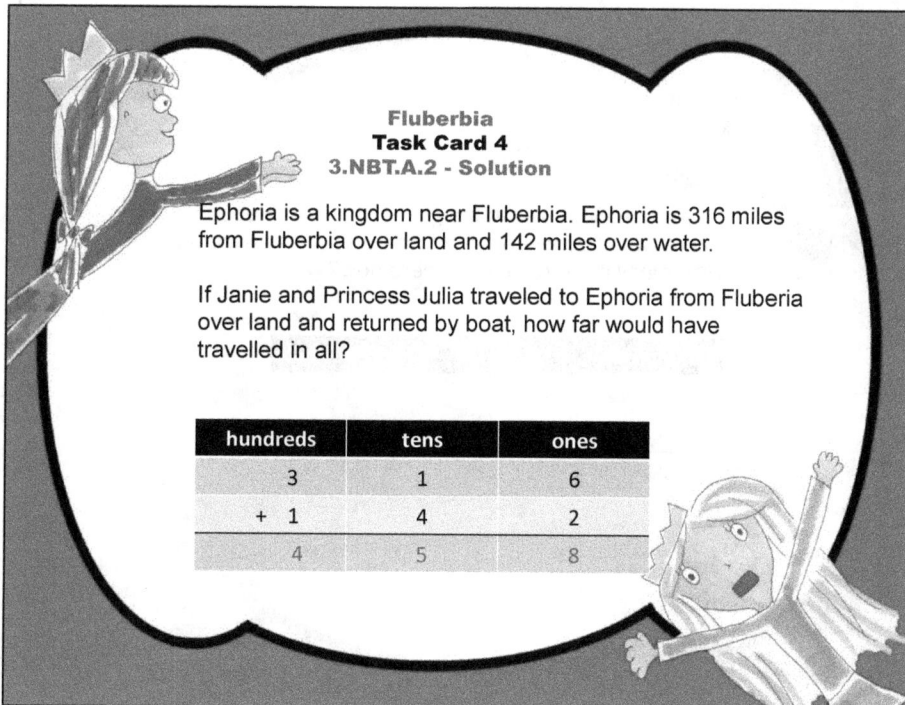

Fluberbia
Task Card 5
3.NBT.A.2

There are 566 rubies in the grand palace of Fluberbia.
There were 125 when the princesses parents were home.
How many more rubies are there now?

hundreds	tens	ones
5	6	6
- 1	2	5

Fluberbia
Task Card 5
3.NBT.A.2 - Solution

There are 566 rubies in the grand palace of Fluberbia.
There were 125 when the princesses parents were home.
How many more rubies are there now?

hundreds	tens	ones
5	6	6
- 1	2	5
4	4	1

Fluberbia
Task Card 7
3.NBT.A.4

a. Write a multiplication number sentence to match this story problem.

Janie helped Princess Claire sort through her emeralds and put the same number in each of 5 boxes. Princess Claire has 65 emeralds. How many can she put in each box?

b. Solve the problem

Fluberbia
Task Card 7
3.NBT.A.4 - Solution

a. Write a multiplication number sentence to match this story problem.

Janie helped Princess Claire sort through her emeralds and put the same number in each of 5 boxes. Princess Claire has 65 emeralds. How many can she put in each box?

5 x _____ = 65

b. Solve the problem

In order to find out how many to put in each box, I have to divide.   65 divided by 5 equals 13.
Check: 13 x 5 = 65

Fluberbia
Task Card 8
3.NBT.A.2

a. Find Janie's mistake and correct it.

```
          5     2
          4     5
    +           9
    _____
          9     6
```

b. Explain your answer.

Fluberbia
Task Card 8
3.NBT.A.2 - Solution

a. Find Janie's mistake and correct it.

```
        1
          5     2
          4     5
    +           9
    _____
    1    0̶9    6
```

b. **Explain your answer.** Janie about regrouping. She added the 5 and the 4 in the tens place, but forgot to bring over the left over 10 from the ones place.

Fluberbia
Task Card 8
3.NBT.A.2

a. **Find Janie's mistake and correct it.**

145 + 34 + 6

```
    1   4   5
    3   4
+   6
─────────────
1   0   8   5
```

b. **Explain your answer.**

Fluberbia
Task Card 8
3.NBT.A.2

a. **Find Janie's mistake and correct it.**

145 + 34 + 6

```
        1
    1   4   5
    3   4
+       6
─────────────
1   8   5
```

b. **Explain your answer.** Janie forgot
about place value, so the answer
is off. I lined up the numbers in
their right place to get my answer.

Fluberbia
Task Card 9
3.NBT.A.2

a. **Find the solution.**

Princess Julia had 12 rubies, 28 sapphires, 6 diamonds and 34 emeralds. How many gems does Princess Julia have in all?

12 + 28 + 6 + 34 = 80 gems in all

b. **Explain your answer.** I could tell by reading the problem that I needed to add. The words "in all" helped me. I lined up the numbers in place value order and added to get 80 gems in all.

Fluberbia
Task Card 9
3.NBT.A.2

a. **Find the solution.**

Princess Julia had 12 rubies, 28 sapphires, 6 diamonds and 34 emeralds. How many gems does Princess Julia have in all?

b. **Explain your answer.**

Fluberbia
Task Card 10
3.NBT.A.2

a. Display the missing digits.

```
    7  3  4            ☐  6  2
 +  8 ☐  6          + 1  7  1
 ─────────           ─────────
  1  5  6  0          7  3  3
```

b. Explain your answers.

Fluberbia
Task Card 10
3.NBT.A.2

a. Display the missing digits.

```
    7  3  4            5  6  2
 +  8  2  6         + 1  7  1
 ─────────           ─────────
  1  5  6  0          7  3  3
```

b. Explain your answer.

Fluberbia
Task Card 11
3.AO.A.3

a. **Write a number sentence to match this story problem and solve.**

Miloph's a bird, a strange one at that, he has two green feet and seven green hats. If he has green feet, his family does too, his mom and his dad and his brother name Lou. He has two sisters and one cousin Pete. Now all of those birds, have how many feet?

b. **Explain your answers.**

Fluberbia
Task Card 11
3.AO.A.3 -- Solution

a. **Write a number sentence to match this story problem and solve.**

Miloph's a bird, a strange one at that, he has two green feet and seven green hats. If he has green feet, his family does too, his mom and his dad and his brother name Lou. He has two sisters and one cousin Pete. Now all of those birds, have how many feet?

(1 mom + 1 dad + 1 brother + 2 sisters + 1 cousin) x 2
(6)   x   2   =   12

b. **Explain your answers.** The easiest way for me to solve this problem is to add all of the people and multiply by the number of feet each has – which is 2.

Fluberbia
Task Card 12
3.AO.A.3

a. **Write a number sentence to match this story problem and solve.**

Auntie Ephoria had the gold crown, but gems it had not and that made her down. The quest was to find, 4 gems for its brim – but what if that tripled? How many then?

b. **Explain your answers.**

Fluberbia
Task Card 12
3.AO.A.3 -- Solution

a. **Write a number sentence to match this story problem and solve.**

Auntie Ephoria had the gold crown, but gems it had not and that made her down. The quest was to find, 4 gems for its brim – but what if that tripled? How many then?

4 x 3 = 12 gems

b. **Explain your answers.** – I multiplied 4 times times 3 because if the gems tripled, I would have to multiple by 4 gems by 3 because triple means 3.

Fluberbia
Task Card 13
3.AO.A.3

a. Write a number sentence to match this story problem and solve.

The diamond, said Miloph, was deep in the snot, but what if 6 more where in the same spot? And what if those 6 each had a mate? How many diamonds would the girls have to take?

6 x 2 = 12 diamonds to take

b. Explain your answers. I know I have to multiply and by reading the problem I know that I begin with 6 diamonds and each as a "mate". Mate means a pair, so I multiply 6 x 2.

Fluberbia
Task Card 14
3.AO.A.3

a. Write a number sentence to match this story problem and solve.

The prince of the Ogres – in the deep gulch of Doom – will have the green gem and they'd reach him soon. They stood on the ridge, and looked down below, and 3 rows of men had picks and had hoes. And each row of 3, had five Ogres in it. How many Ogres would they meet when all finished?

b. Explain your answers.

Fluberbia
Task Card 14
3.AO.A.3 – Solution

a. **Write a number sentence to match this story problem and solve.**

The prince of the Ogres – in the deep gulch of Doom – will have the green gem and they'd reach him soon. They stood on the ridge, and looked down below, and 3 rows of men had picks and had hoes. And each row of 3, had five Ogres in it. How many Ogres would they meet when all finished?

3 rows   x   5 Ogres   =   15 Ogres in all

b. **Explain your answers.** I know I have to multiple because there are three rows with five Ogres in each. That is 3 x 5 or 5 + 5 + 5

Fluberbia
Task Card 15
3.AO.A.3

a. **Write a number sentence to match this story problem and solve.**

Janie and Claire needed to eat, when they came across trees with apples for treats. There were 3 trees, with apples for eating, they each picked 11 – and they began feasting.

b. **Explain your answers.**

Task Card 15
3.AO.A.3 – Solution

a. **Write a number sentence to match this story problem and solve.**

Janie and Claire needed to eat, when they came across trees with apples for treats. There were 3 trees, with apples for eating, they each picked 11 – and they began feasting.

2 girls x 11 apples = 22 apples in all

b. **Explain your answers.** This one tried to trick me. It talks about 3 trees, but I don't need that information. The problem asks how many apples in all if each person picks 11 and there are 2 people, so 2 times 11 equals 22

Fluberbia
Task Card 16
3.AO.A.3 – Solution

Find the products. Draw a picture to help if you need to.

1) 2 x 4 x 2
2) 3 x 2 x 3
3) 4 x 2 x 2
4) 5 x 2 x 2
5) 2 x 6 x 2
6) 3 x 2 x 4

Fluberbia
Task Card 16
3.AO.A.3 – Solution

Find the products. Draw a picture to help if you need to.

1) 2 x 4 x 2 =
   16
2) 3 x 2 x 3 =
   18
3) 4 x 2 x 2 =
   16
4) 5 x 2 x 2 =
   20
5) 2 x 6 x 2 =
   24

Fluberbia
Task Card 17
3.AO.A.3

Find the products. Draw a picture to help if you need to.

1) 6 x 3 x 1
2) 6 x 3 x 3
3) 5 x 2 x 1
4) 5 x 3 x 2
5) 5 x 2 x 3
6) 2 x 2 x 5
7) 4 x 3 x 3

Task Card 17
3.AO.A.3 – Solution

Find the products. Draw a picture to help if you need to.

1) 6 x 3 x 1 = 18

2) 6 x 3 x 2 = 36

3) 5 x 2 x 1 = 10

4) 5 x 3 x 2 = 30

5) 5 x 2 x 3 = 30

6) 2 x 2 x 5 = 20

7) 4 x 3 x 3 = 36

Fluberbia
Task Card 18
3.AO.A.3

Write the missing number and solve.

(2 x 7) x 4 = 2 x (7 x ___)

3 x (4 x 6) = (3 x ___) x 6

(5 x 3) x 2 = 3 x (2 x ___)

2 x (7 x ___) = (2 x 7) x 3

Write the missing number and solve.

$(2 \times 7) \times 4 = 2 \times (7 \times \mathbf{4})$
$= 56$

$3 \times (4 \times 6) = (3 \times \mathbf{4}) \times 6$
$= 72$

$(5 \times 3) \times 2 = 3 \times (2 \times \mathbf{5})$
$= 30$

$2 \times (7 \times \mathbf{3}) = (2 \times 7) \times 3$
$= 42$

Solve.

1) $6 \times 7 =$ ___
2) $8 \times 9 =$ ___
3) $4 \times 5 =$ ___
4) $6 \times 9 =$ ___
5) $8 \times 7 =$ ___
6) $3 \times 9 =$ ___
7) $6 \times 8 =$ ___

Fluberbia
Task Card 19
3.AO.A.3 - Solution

Solve.

1) 6 x 7 = 42
2) 8 x 9 = 72
3) 4 x 5 = 20
4) 6 x 9 = 54
5) 8 x 7 = 56
6) 3 x 9 = 27
7) 6 x 8 = 48